DEPARTMENT OF THE ENVIRONMENT
(Inner Cities Directorate)

GREENING CITY SITES

Case Studies of Good Practice in Urban Regeneration

Prepared for the Department of the Environment by:
JURUE, a division of ECOTEC Research and Consulting Ltd.

DEPARTMENT·OF
THE·ENVIRONMENT

LONDON: HER MAJESTY'S STATIONERY OFFICE

© Crown copyright 1987
   First published 1987

ISBN 0 11 752013 6

Preface

This report was commissioned by the Inner Cities Directorate of the Department of the Environment as one of a series of studies to disseminate aspects of 'good practice' in the development and management of projects to improve conditions within urban areas.

The report has been prepared by a team of researchers with JURUE, a division of ECOTEC Research and Consulting Ltd, in association with William Gillespie and Partners, who have provided advice on landscape design matters, and Joan Davidson, an environmental consultant, who has advised the team on aspects of community involvement in environmental projects.

In preparing this report the Consultants have relied heavily on the time and information provided by the very large numbers of individuals who have been consulted. For this, and the many positive and helpful suggestions received, the Consultants are indebted.

Contents

Part 1

INTRODUCTION

Introduction

Dereliction, eyesores, underused and contaminated land are both a symptom and a cause of the wider problems of urban areas. They have arisen partly as a consequence of population loss, employment loss and economic decline. They in turn contribute to low levels of private sector investment through worsening the image and hence business confidence within these areas. Arguably the spiral of decline has been accelerated by increased awareness of environmental conditions that has led both people and business to shun extensive areas of our cities.

But the picture is by no means all gloomy. Much has been done to reclaim and improve sites for the benefit of those living and working in urban areas. Considerable energy, resources and commitment have been expended, often in the face of daunting and large scale problems, and this provides the basis for drawing lessons on 'good practice'. This is the purpose of this document. It is hoped that these lessons will be applied to the major environmental improvements tasks that remain to be tackled.

The document presents a synthesis of the key features and lessons derived from successful projects and a series of case studies. Much of the case material used in this document derives from an earlier study undertaken by JURUE which evaluated environmental projects funded under the Urban Programme (Department of the Environment, 1986). Each project has been carefully examined, the consultants have talked to those directly affected by the projects and those involved in their implementation. In particular, systematic surveys of users and those living in the vicinity of projects have been undertaken for most of the projects and the views of those canvassed have been a major influence upon the consultants' assessments of 'good practice'.

The audience

It is intended that the document should be of value to a wide range of different groups and individuals. These include:

- Local authority officers involved with the development of environmental projects in urban areas.

- Voluntary groups and other grassroots organisations actually or potentially involved in improvement projects.

- Private sector organisations and individual companies operating from and owning land within urban areas.

- Charitable trusts and other potential sources of funding.

- Public sector land and property owners.

- Officers, civil servants and politicians within local authorities and central government concerned with managing change and resources in urban areas.

Inevitably, the needs of these groups are extremely diverse so the synthesis and case studies cannot hope to satisfy them all fully. However, together they present some ideas and draw out lessons, many of which may, with the benefit of hindsight, seem obvious, but which have, in some instances, been learnt through bitter experience. It is hoped that these hard learned lessons will help inform those considering, or currently responsible for, initiating and undertaking environmental improvement schemes. For those requiring a better insight into the action most likely to bring about improvements, there is no substitute for a visit and discussions with those directly involved with similar projects. There is also a growing body of helpful resource material for the enthusiast, specialist and generalist and helpful references are provided at the end of the report.

Good practice

Many aspects of good practice are discussed in this document. These include:

- responsiveness to local needs and opportunities;

1

- good management and the resolution of complex problems;
- innovative and attractive designs;
- drawing together of a wide variety of resources;
- adaptability.

Some of the projects described and referred to have been particularly successful in some but not all these facets of good practice. Figure 1 indicates the aspects of 'good practice' illustrated by the case study projects. It must be stressed that these aspects extend well beyond the primarily visual criteria conventionally applied to judge environmental improvements.

The case studies have been selected because they illustrate aspects of 'good practice' and have also met three key criteria. These are:

(i) benefits have been derived by those living and working in inner urban areas;

(ii) objectives specified for the project have been attained;

(iii) each project was cost effective compared with projects of a similar nature and the expenditure and specification were appropriate for the objectives set.

The projects are not necessarily 'best practice' nor, by any means, the only examples of good practice. Rather, the selection of environmental improvement projects has been deliberately drawn to embrace a wide variety of different approaches, uses, sizes and contexts.

They range from the most modest 'corner' site to the provision of a town park, and from improvements to a car park to the provision of several hectares of amenity open space in a clearance area. Each provides useful lessons which highlight the opportunities and hurdles that require consideration in carrying out such projects. It is important, however, to bear in mind that there is no single 'correct' approach to environmental improvement. What is successful in one context may be inappropriate in another, even where circumstances are apparently similar.

The projects
For convenience, the projects which are presented as case studies, have been grouped into six categories:

- Public open space for passive leisure use and walkways.
- Active and organised recreation projects.
- Housing related improvements.
- Visual enhancements.
- Projects in industrial and commercial areas.
- Voluntary sector projects.

Each case study is presented in Part III of the report but reference is made to individual projects, by name, throughout Part II. All the projects are situated within urban areas, many in areas suffering from very high levels of deprivation. They all involve improvements, either visual or through allowing new uses on previously disused, underused and derelict land. Nearly all have received financial support from the Urban Programme. Over and above this some of the projects have benefited from the efforts and creative resources of the voluntary sector, co-operation and finance from the private sector, and inputs from labour employed on Manpower Services Commission (MSC) programmes.

Overall, the bulk of the projects have been initiated by local authorities. More particularly, individual local authority departments have played a central role in identifying potential projects and undertaking the necessary design, implementation and management work. Indeed, the selection of case studies reflects the dominant role that local authorities have played in this kind of environmental improvement work. However, many of the projects discussed have involved the voluntary sector in initiation, design, implementation, and in some cases, maintenance. They illustrate the key role that voluntary organisations can play in ensuring that projects are responsive to local needs and in undertaking and managing improvement works.

Figure 1

Aspects of 'Good Practice' illustrated by the Case Studies

		Windmill Hill City Farm	Windmill Grove Garden	Hackney Grove Garden	Lever Edge	Bexley Square	Electric Avenue	Trenchfield Mill	Riverside Park / Trenthaugh	Derwenthaugh / Fish Quay	Noble's Quay	Baylis Road	Exchange Station Car Park	Bansteads	Broughton High and Ascension	Hylton Dene	Black Patch	Potternewton Park	Green's Gardens	Cannon Street Park	Hatfield Road	Sheepwash	Hendon Cliff Top	Town Centre Park
Responsiveness to local needs and opportunities	Public consultation		•			•						•					•	•				•	•	•
	Response to special group needs		•	•		•						•						•			•			
	Good use of existing features				•		•	•	•							•			•	•	•		•	•
	Associated economic effects	•			•	•	•	•	•		•		•											•
Good Management and resolution of 'complex' problems	Linked to strategic policy goals				•	•	•	•	•		•		•				•	•		•	•	•		•
	Strong co-ordination between departments and agencies					•	•	•	•								•		•					
	Involves environmental education	•	•									•		•	•	•			•			•		
	Innovative approaches to maintenance		•	•											•	•								
	Re-use of materials	•										•		•				•						•
	Successful planting regimes		•				•			•										•	•			
	Successful combination of activities		•				•							•	•		•		•	•	•		•	•
	Low maintenance requirements				•	•	•	•						•	•	•	•			•		•	•	•
	Strong visual impact		•		•		•		•	•	•	•	•	•	•	•	•			•				•
Innovative and attractive design	Private sector contribution											•												
	Community and voluntary sector involvement	•		•		•				•				•			•	•	•	•		•		
	Diversity of funding	•	•							•				•			•	•	•	•				
Adaptability	Meets multiple objectives	•		•		•				•	•		•	•					•				•	•
	Scope for further improvement	•	•		•	•	•					•		•	•	•	•			•	•			

3

Part II

LESSONS FOR GOOD PRACTICE

Lessons for Good Practice

This part of the report draws together the findings from the case studies and highlights 'good practice' lessons. It comprises five sections.

Section 1, 'Making Things Happen', discusses the ways in which projects have been identified and the factors that influence the successful choice of sites and improvement specifications. Emphasis is given to the contribution that the community can make to improvement projects and ways in which they have been effectively involved.

Once improvements are established it is critical that they are maintained and managed so that they continue to meet their objectives. This is particularly important in the face of severe constraints on public sector revenue resources. Section 2, 'Making Things Last', identifies the factors that can facilitate maintenance and the ways in which it has been achieved in the case studies.

The achievements of environmental improvement projects are frequently influenced by design factors. Indeed quite detailed design features can significantly affect both the perceptions and the use of improvement projects. Section 3, 'Design Ideas' discusses some of the alternative design approaches, the design features that have been particularly successful in the case studies and some of the principles underlying effective design.

The scale of environmental improvement tasks facing the urban areas of Britain and the constraints on public expenditure require very careful consideration of issues of cost-effectiveness. The variety of objectives set for environmental improvements and the range of contexts within which they are set mean that straightforward measures of cost effectiveness, such as cost per unit of land are, in themselves, insufficient. Instead careful consideration needs to be given to the appropriate level of treatment, the implications for after care and the ways in which the wider community can be involved. Section 4, 'Getting the Most from Limited Resources', discusses these issues.

The final section of this synthesis, Section 5, 'Learning by Doing', considers ways in which the progress of improvements can be monitored in order that, when necessary, action is taken to ensure that they continue to meet their objectives and to inform future choices and approaches to environmental improvement.

1 Making things happen

The process of initiating and implementing environmental improvements involves two critical choices: what sites and what activities? In particular a number of aspects are important:

(a) the initial push.

(b) ways in which resources have been pulled together.

(c) how projects have been managed during implementation.

(d) the role of the community and voluntary organisations.

(e) the criteria affecting the choice of sites.

(f) factors influencing what activities can best be accommodated.

The initial push

A large number of factors have led to the improvements described in this document being undertaken. They include, most importantly:

- expressions of interest by the community;

- identification of problems and opportunities during the local planning process;

- the needs of local authority service departments;

- the ideas of individual officers and members;

- the reproduction of projects developed elsewhere.

The factors that have most often been linked to successful projects are:

- Local pressure and commitment. This was, for example, important at LEVER EDGE and BAYLIS ROAD.

- The enthusiasm and determination of individuals or groups within or outside the local authorities to undertake the work, a factor clearly illustrated at WINDMILL HILL CITY FARM and HACKNEY GROVE GARDEN.

- Skilful management to ensure that ideas and proposals have been prepared to capitalise on resources when they become available. For example, having the ELECTRIC AVENUE project approved and 'ready to go' enabled an underspend on capital budget allocations to be taken up, effectively bringing the project forward.

- Careful management to combine the skills and resources of a wide range of specialists. This has been especially important to the success of projects such as HACKNEY GROVE GARDEN.

- The pursuit of environmental and economic objectives, particularly when related to broader strategic goals. For instance, the goal of retaining commercial interest in central Sunderland through environmental improvements provided the context for TOWN CENTRE PARK; the improvements to EXCHANGE STATION both reduces the detrimental impact of an underused prime site and presents a favourable impression to potential developers; and, DERWENTHAUGH RIVERSIDE PARK is only one component of improvements in the vicinity of the Tyne.

The achievements of projects have been more disappointing when improvements have been focussed on the most 'convenient' sites (such as local authority owned land) and where projects have arisen as a result of bartering between service departments, each viewing the improvements in terms of narrow departmental responsibilities.

Pulling resources together

All the improvements described in this document required public sector funding. Very few projects have the potential to generate significant revenues. Public sector resources are limited and the achievements of pulling together resources has been critical to the success of many of the projects reviewed.

There are many aspects to this process. GREEN'S GAR-

DENS and BLACK PATCH have illustrated strong co-operation between local authority departments. HACK-NEY GROVE GARDEN and LEVER EDGE have drawn in expertise and/or labour from the voluntary sector. Manpower Services Commission labour has been utilised from both Youth Training Schemes and the Community Programme, for example, GREEN'S GARDENS and WINDMILL HILL CITY FARM. BAYLIS ROAD benefited from a Sports Council grant and the private sector has been involved through licence and access agreements, sponsorship, donations, and in the case of ELECTRIC AVENUE, direct contributions. GREEN'S GARDENS provides a particularly good example of a project combining different sources of funding.

At the technical level, resources available from the Department of the Environment's Derelict Land Grant have been combined with those available from the Urban Programme within a single contract specification to enable a higher standard of reclamation. Good use has also been made of advice from agencies such as the Nature Conservancy Council, as at HYLTON DENE.

Certain projects have also helped generate commitment to environmental improvement works by agencies such as British Rail (ELECTRIC AVENUE) and British Waterways Board. Indeed, the successful projects have demonstrated the value of improvements, and, in showing what can be done, helped provide the impetus at member, officer and community levels for further initiatives.

Managing implementation

Many of the projects referred to are complex, making good management practices essential to their success. Good management practices are also particularly valuable when the time scale for improvement works is long.

For many projects good planning is critical in order to ensure that the momentum of improvement is maintained, so that, for example, planting seasons are not lost. Many different arrangements have been adopted for implementing improvement works and there are no necessarily 'correct' mechanisms. However, close liaison is essential between project managers, designers, beneficiaries, contract negotiators, contractors and those who are likely to be responsible for maintenance. Responsibilities for overall progress and financial monitoring should not be diffused. Indeed, projects benefit from having a 'champion', a key person to co-ordinate inputs to the project and take responsibility for its progress (for example, BLACK PATCH). In the case of projects undertaken by local authority departments it is helpful to have a named officer who is responsible for implementation.

Whenever paid MSC and volunteer labour is used, very careful planning and management is required to define the different tasks and responsibilities and oversee the work on a day to day basis.

Community involvement

The principal objective of most of the projects reviewed in this document is to improve living and working conditions within older urban areas. This objective has been most effectively met by ensuring that projects meet the needs of those most directly affected by them. Community involvement has helped in this respect and taken many guises.

Pressure and complaints from residents and voluntary organisations has drawn attention to the need for environmental improvements in several case studies. This is illustrated by the LEVER EDGE, HACKNEY GROVE GARDEN, WINDMILL HILL CITY FARM, and BAYLIS ROAD case studies. In GREEN'S GARDENS local conservation work, supported by a memorial fund, provided the initial impetus for improvements.

Residents and local interest groups became involved at the planning stage of the BANSTEADS through a public consultation exercise and this has influenced the types of facilities provided. An especially good example of the way that the community can be encouraged to become involved is the BLACK PATCH project where the council appointment of a community landscape architect has enabled close consultations with residents on this housing estate.

Involvement of the voluntary sector in planning and design work is not common, but this occurred in HACKNEY GROVE GARDEN where an organisation, Free Form, a community arts trust, was engaged to undertake a feasibility study.

Another mechanism by which the involvement of the community has been encouraged is through voluntary sector and technical aid agencies that have provided advice to residents and other groups wishing to become involved in improvement projects.

Several projects have engaged volunteers in implementation. These include WINDMILL HILL CITY FARM, HACKNEY GROVE GARDEN and an innovative project in Manchester involving the free distribution of bulbs to voluntary organisations and schools for planting on public land. Indeed several of the case studies have involved schools in implementation, for example, SHEEPWASH, and patients from local hospitals (HACKNEY GROVE GARDEN). This may have the effect of reducing subsequent vandalism as well as meeting environmental education objectives.

At LEVER EDGE the voluntary sector has also been involved in after care and maintenance. This important role is discussed in more detail in Section 2 below.

Community involvement has been of benefit in all the cases where it has taken place. The projects have been more closely tailored to local needs and the commitment and pride generated has been linked to lower levels of vandalism than might otherwise have occurred.

There are a number of other mechanisms by which community involvement may be encouraged.
- Public or private sector support for agencies such as the British Trust for Conservation Volunteers and

Groundwork Trusts, which have been successful in encouraging community participation in environmental improvement.

- The establishment of a forum of voluntary agencies to discuss urban environmental issues with local authority officers and councillors. An example of this has been used for project initiation and consultation purposes in Nottingham.

- Direct financial support to voluntary agencies for the design and implementation of schemes.

- Private sector support for innovation approaches to environmental improvements. The AMA/ Sainsbury Trust's Derelict Land Initiative has shown that relatively small amounts of financial assistance achieve positive community spinoffs. Seven grants given for the innovative use of derelict and underused land have helped projects to secure other funding support and to generate community interest and involvement in planning and afteruse. The flexibility of the assistance has been particularly beneficial. In one case a grant, given initially for revenue expenditure was subsequently used for a capital investment. The timescales for expenditure were also extended. This flexibility provides a contrast to the rigidity of other funding regimes.

The choice of sites

Resources for urban environmental improvements are limited and very difficult choices are necessary when considering where improvements can best be undertaken. Factors that have influenced 'good practice' in terms of site selection include:

- The numbers of potential beneficiaries either living, travelling or working in the vicinity of improvements. Almost all of the projects referred to in this report have been well chosen in this respect. They contrast with some projects that are isolated and unlikely to be frequently seen or used.

- Where improvements have addressed the most evident and marked environmental conditions within the immediate vicinity or neighbourhood, their value has been more readily appreciated. The BANSTEADS and HENDON CLIFF TOP projects are good examples of this. The failure to adopt such an approach will, at best, decrease the value of any improvements made and, at worst, provoke cynicism amongst those supposed to benefit.

- Where the choice of sites and improvement works accords with the priorities of those living and working in the area. Here, again, a sound understanding of local needs is required. There will, for example, be little benefit in undertaking apparently expensive landscaping schemes in the vicinity of housing that is itself in need of urgent repair or

improvement. It is, therefore, particularly important to undertake internal and external housing improvement works together, wherever possible, (for example, BLACK PATCH). It is also important that improvements should be made in such a manner that the site is responsive to changing needs and priorities within the community, as is well illustrated at POTTERNEWTON PARK.

- Where the improvements can be clearly linked to a concerted and planned effort to improve conditions in the wider area. It is important that where there is evidently need for further improvements in the vicinity of the improvement works already undertaken, the envisaged improvements and developments should, as far as possible, be presented publicly with a time scale over which it is hoped that they will be achieved. This has been done at SHEEPWASH. Currently, there is little or no awareness of a national commitment to improve environmental conditions in older urban areas. This may be difficult to achieve but at a local level improvements should be set within a plan that should be both realisable and understandable. Publicity should be given to these efforts so as to raise awareness and confidence in an area. Where appropriate information boards should be erected on individual sites. The DERWENTHAUGH RIVERSIDE PARK and TRENCHERFIELD MILL projects are examples of well publicised improvements within wider programmes of work (Derwenthaugh IIA and Wigan Pier respectively) which illustrate some of these principles.

The choice of activities

The second difficult set of choices concern what should be accommodated on the improved site. Again, the types and combinations of activities have been most successful when they have reflected local priorities and taken account of local needs. These are extremely diverse and include:

- Young children require secure and safe environments, preferably overlooked by housing and in areas physically separated from more active recreation areas. This can be achieved by careful siting and design, as illustrated at HATFIELD ROAD, CANNON STREET PARK and the BANSTEADS.

- The elderly are likely to prefer quiet and secure areas, comfortable seating and where possible an interesting outlook. This has been achieved in the TOWN CENTRE PARK, NOBLE'S QUAY/FISH QUAY and HATFIELD ROAD.

- The active teenager will require space and robust facilities such as kick-about areas. When organised by schools and sports clubs detailed design, quality and management will be important, (for example, BAYLIS ROAD and BROUGHTON HIGH AND ASCENSION).

- Almost all age groups can benefit from open space for passive recreation, as shown by HENDON CLIFF TOP and SHEEPWASH in particular.

- The pedestrian and shopper will require improvements that are straightforward, that accommodate 'desire lines' and that are practical. A good example of this is TOWN CENTRE PARK.

- Within housing areas improvements should take account of the needs for private and semi-public space, as has been attempted at BLACK PATCH.

- The potential developer will be influenced by the visual impact, by the quality of the improvements, and by assurances that the improvements will remain. EXCHANGE STATION and DERWENTHAUGH RIVERSIDE PARK illustrate contrasting approaches that may favourably impress potential developers.

- The industrialist and traders will require improvements that enhance the attractiveness of their locations and improve them functionally. Benefits of this type have occurred on ELECTRIC AVENUE and NOBLE'S QUAY/FISH QUAY.

- Schools and environmental groups can benefit from the educational opportunities provided by interesting and varied environments, (as has occurred at SHEEPWASH). Benefits will be more widely felt if interpretative material is provided.

What is provided will depend upon the objectives for the improvements, local needs, the physical context and the opportunities presented by the site. All of the projects referred to here have successfully taken account of these factors. Some have skilfully combined the needs of the different groups described above. For example:

- Dual use by schools and community has been achieved in BROUGHTON HIGH AND ASCENSION.

- TOWN CENTRE PARK combines the needs of pedestrians and shoppers with the provision of attractive meeting places.

- Active and passive recreation activities have been successfully combined in HATFIELD ROAD, GREEN'S GARDENS and CANNON STREET.

- A total of thirteen different activities have been accommodated on the BANSTEADS and many within the quite confined spaces of HACKNEY GROVE GARDEN, and WINDMILL HILL CITY FARM.

- Park refurbishments have led to the provision of new facilities, these include basketball courts in POTTERNEWTON PARK, in response to changing community needs.

Key conclusions

(i) It is important to involve the community in decisions concerning what should be done. Where possible the community should take the lead.

(ii) Financial and staff resources can be drawn in from a variety of sources and creatively combined.

(iii) The time scale could be long, but continual progress towards 'targets' may be necessary in order to maintain momentum.

(iv) The strong commitment of individuals within and outside authorities may be required, as will a wide range of skills and experience.

(v) Technical aid groups can help by enabling the voluntary sector to assist in the improvement process.

(vi) Within a small area it is best to deal with the worst site or eyesore first, if possible.

(vii) Isolated and infrequently used areas that are not already a focus of activity and have little prospect of becoming so should be given low priority.

(viii) Improvements should be set within a plan, which should be realisable and understandable to those that are meant to benefit.

(ix) The priorities adopted should be common sense and reflect community aspirations.

(x) Whilst it is difficult to successfully integrate a wide variety of uses and user groups within one scheme, it can and often should be done.

2   Making things last

The previous section of the report discussed how environmental improvements could be made to happen. Equally important is the task of making the improvements last and ensuring that they continue to meet the objectives set and the needs of beneficiaries. Three factors underly this task:

- environmental improvements are fragile; if not managed and maintained properly they can quickly become unkempt, undervalued, disrespected and, eventually, eyesores.

- improvements are never really complete, not only will they change physically as the vegetation matures, but the use of them will change reflecting wider social changes and priorities.

- management and aftercare usually requires labour and revenue rather than capital inputs. In general, public sector expenditure, including the Urban Programme, has given priority to capital rather than revenue expenditure. This, coupled with constraints on local authority expenditure, has placed a premium upon exploring innovative and low cost approaches to maintenance and designing projects so as to reduce maintenance requirements.

This section of the report explores some of the principles underlying the assessment of aftercare requirements, indicates the ways in which the community has been successfully involved in management and maintenance, and discusses some of the design and organisational factors that make maintenance and aftercare easier.

Assessing aftercare requirements
Constraints on revenue expenditure, illustrated for example, by the level of maintenance work falling short of that considered necessary by the implementing authority in several of the case studies, emphasises the importance of considering aftercare

requirements at the design stage. Many factors will affect these requirements, including:

- Planting regimes.

- The use of the site.

- The use of 'hard' and 'soft' landscaping.

The approach that is required to assess and cost these requirements involves:

- The appraisal of maintenance and management implications of the constituent parts of the design. A recently completed study by Handley and Bulmer (1986) assessed the resource requirements of the maintenance of a wide range of land uses and appropriate management regimes.

- The assessment of the scope for community involvement.

Essentially, the approach to assessing the aftercare requirements of urban environmental improvements should be analogous to the cost-in-use assessments made of buildings at the design stage. In so far as trade-off's exist between initial capital and future revenue expenditure these should be explored. But these trade-offs are not straightforward, high cost projects will not necessarily lead to low maintenance costs, indeed the reverse is often the case. Once these trade-offs have been explored in broad terms it will be necessary to prepare a management plan for the vegetation. This should include a clear allocation of responsibilities.

Figure 2 indicates in broad terms the levels of maintenance and management required for the case study projects. It illustrates the wide range of costs per unit of land required.

The scope for community involvement
There are several prerequisites and mechanisms through which the community can be encouraged to

FIGURE 2: Relative costs of maintenance and aftercare management

Category	Project	Costs of Maintenance and Management	Notes
Public Open Space for Passive Leisure	Town Centre Park	●●	Limited maintenance undertaken due to financial constraints
	Hendlon Cliff Top	●	
	Sheepwash	Not Known	Maintenance incorporated in the development costs of Sheepwash Urban Park
Active and Organised Recreation Projects	Hatfield Road	●●●●	Maintenance costs of park have risen since refurbishment project implemented
	Cannon Street Park	●●	
	Potternewton Park	●	
Housing Related Improvements	Black Patch	Not Known	Maintenance costs unlikely to have increased because of the improvements
	Green's Gardens	●●	
	Hylton Dene	●	
	Broughton High and Ascension	Not Known	Management costs include provision of caretaker on site
	Bansteads	●●●●●	High costs due to heavy usage and some vandalism
Visual Enhancements	Exchange Station Car Park	Not Known	Costs not calculated for individual sites
	Baylis Road	Not Known	
	Nobles Quay/Fish Quay	●	Limited maintenance undertaken due to financial constraints
Projects in Industrial and Commercial Areas	Derwenthaugh Riverside Park	Not Known	Maintenance currently the responsibility of contractors
	Trencherfield Mill	●	
	Electric Avenue	Not Known	Additional costs since improvement work low
	Bexley Square	Not Known	Undertaken as part of general street cleansing and maintenance programme.
Voluntary Sector Projects	Level Edge	●	Schoolchildren and parents involved in maintenance. Parents contribute to maintenance costs
	Hackney Grove Garden	●●●●	Costs include the organisation and staging of events. Volunteers assist in maintenance work.
	Windmill Hill City Farm	●●●●●	Costs include management staff

KEY   Management and Maintenance Costs (Annual Cost Per Square Metre)
- ● less than £0.05
- ●● £0.06 – £0.25
- ●●● £0.26 – £0.50
- ●●●● £0.51 – £1.00
- ●●●●● greater than £1.00

become involved in the management and after care of urban environmental improvements. These include:

- *The recognition that the role local people can play in caring for green areas in towns and cities is important.* Projects which require a high labour input during implementation and for aftercare provide an opportunity for local participation and involve-

ment. However, as there is likely to be competition for volunteer time careful supervision is likely to be required. It should be remembered that volunteers generally prefer to implement rather than manage improvements. HACKNEY GROVE GARDEN illustrates how events and activities can be creatively combined with maintenance tasks in order to sustain interest and enthusiasm. Volunteers can

13

also be helpful in managing informal or 'unofficial' urban open space. These tracts of land, where access has been restricted and which have been gradually colonised by indigenous species, offer potential for creatively managed local amenity areas. The British Trust for Conservation Volunteers in Leeds has shown what can be done. A low cost project was initiated in the Kirkstall Valley and local people have been sucessfully involved in the management of an area of overgrown landscape. Similarly, HYLTON DENE provides an opportunity to bring into more beneficial use an existing 'unofficial' area with the help of local volunteers in its maintenance. Leeds Leisure Services Department involved school children in the BANSTEADS by holding a competition to name the area. In Sunderland, interpretive class room displays were used to raise awareness and interest in maintaining the improvements at HYLTON DENE, and several projects, including SHEEPWASH and LEVER EDGE, have involved schoolchildren in planting trees and shrubs.

- *Providing an individual to liaise with the community to generate local commitment to maintenance and management.* In Bradford, for example, an environmental warden has been funded on a public housing estate; in Sandwell, a community landscape architect continues to spend time at BLACK PATCH; and, Sholver, a run down public housing estate near Oldham, is regularly visited by rangers from the Oldham and Rochdale Groundwork Trust. In each of these examples the awareness and involvement of the local community in the management of this environment has been raised. This is reflected in quite straightforward ways such as the reliable reporting of damage and the deterioration of improvements.

- *Clear information,* including boards or signs, explaining the purpose of the improvements and the future aims for the area illustrate commitment which can also help increase community conciousness and interest in the works.

Factors that make maintenance easier: design
There are aspects of design which contribute to the lasting quality of urban environmental improvements. At the planning stage it is important that ways in which design features can aid or reduce maintenance are considered. Some examples of how design can influence maintenance are suggested below:

- Where grass is to be mown the design should allow this to be carried out easily beside footpaths, hard landscape features and particularly around areas of planting. SHEEPWASH provides a good example of thoughtful design in this respect.

- A few semi-mature trees or the dense planting of trees and shrubs, as at CANNON STREET PARK, can both achieve immediate visual impact and are less likely to attract vandalism than well spaced standard trees.

- Close planting may have low short term maintenance requirements but these may increase once the trees and shrubs mature.

- Retaining walls around raised flowerbeds (TRENCHERFIELD MILL) and kickabout areas (BAYLIS ROAD and POTTERNEWTON PARK) need to be durable enough to withstand heavy use and reduce the need for repairs.

- Footpaths need to be situated along 'desire lines'. If footpaths are to be constructed of hard materials then this may best be undertaken after desired directions have been defined.

- Designs that allow for cropping or sheep grazing may have lower maintenance costs and even provide some income, (for example, WINDMILL HILL CITY FARM).

Also, as evidenced by several of the case studies, improvements can take a considerable period to undertake and their use and the perceptions and needs of those in the vicinity will change. Thus it is important that the designs should be able to accommodate further improvements and revisions (for example, CANNON STREET PARK, HYLTON DENE, and HENDON CLIFF TOP) and cater for current demands whilst being part of wider programmes of improvement, as illustrated by SHEEPWASH.

Factors that make maintenance easier: organisation
It needs to be clear from the design stage who is responsible for the maintenance and management of the improvement. The resource implications should also be known at that stage.

Where community involvement and commitment to management have been obtained it is important to delineate responsibility. Supervision of volunteers will be needed and sometimes this will require specialist skills and experience.

Maintenance agreements covering two or three years included within contracted out improvement works, as has occurred at DERWENTHAUGH RIVERSIDE PARK, can be helpful in deferring calls on local authority revenue resources.

Key conclusions

(i)   Improvements should never be viewed as complete. Whatever approach is adopted aftercare is of central importance and integral to the success of projects.

(ii)   Design approaches can reduce the maintenance and aftercare requirements but by no means eliminate them.

(iii)   The community can play an important role in aftercare especially where the initial improvements are directly responsive to their needs.

(iv)   Improvements should be adaptable and able to take account of changing tastes and community needs.

(v)   There are innovative mechanisms that have successfully involved the community and can be linked to reductions in vandalism.

3   Design ideas

There are two main criteria that are used to assess the design characteristics of the project; what looks good, especially in the eyes of those living and working in the vicinity, and what is well used.

The design issues centre on:

(a) The desirability of 'natural' or more 'manicured' environments.

(b) The merits of 'traditional' or varied 'soft' landscapes.

(c) The merits of different kinds of 'hard' landscaping.

(d) Ways of successfully combining different landscapes and activities.

(e) Making the most of opportunities and changes.

(f) Re-use of materials.

'Natural' and 'Manicured' Environments

A number of the case studies illustrate these contrasting approaches. The former emphasis provides the impression of the environment reverting to its 'natural' state and allows for the establishment of native flora, fauna and wildlife. The latter approach provides a contrast to the natural state both visually and in terms of vegetation.

The main benefits of natural environments are that they can:

- bring the feel of the countryside to those living in urban areas;

- provide opportunities for understanding the natural environment;

- have low maintenance implications, if straightforward schemes;

- provide habits that conserve wildlife.

The disadvantages sometimes include:

- perception as insecure and unsuitable for casual use;

- need for careful management.

It should be stressed that 'natural' environments, in the sense used here, are not necessarily the same as the environments that would re-establish if the sites were left for prolonged periods of time. Nor are they necessarily low cost, particularly if they are established rapidly and intensively used for recreation and interpretation.

The main benefits of more 'manicured' environments are that they can:

- provide striking visual impact;

- give a strong impression of care and attention and thus may contribute to civic pride;

- be designed to accommodate different needs and activities.

Against this, the major possible disadvantage is that of:

- high maintenance costs.

In some respects these approaches need not be strict alternatives. As discussed more fully in Section 4, improvements can be made to markedly different levels. Low cost 'natural' approaches, at HENDON CLIFF TOP for example, have been as successful as the more intensive and expensive 'manicured' improvements at TOWN CENTRE PARK, though the location and purposes were clearly very different. Indeed, local perceptions of improvements will depend upon the state of the environment prior to the improvement works. Low cost improvement can be highly valued where they address the most marked and prominent local eyesores.

However, whilst 'natural' low cost schemes can bring about valued improvements they are unlikely in themselves to significantly change the image of older industrial areas.

The merits of 'traditional' or varied 'soft' landscapes

The urban environment is never static and it is appropriate that the soft landscaping employed should reflect both the usage and the traditions of the areas in which they are set. In many cases a traditional or more uniform landscape may be the most appropriate. An example of this is TOWN CENTRE PARK where the formal planting serves as a counterpoint to the modern facade of the nearby leisure centre. The formal layout of tall standard and semi-mature trees in BEXLEY SQUARE reflects the conservation area status of the square.

On sites where the main forms of recreational activity are of an active nature then grassed areas are often the most appropriate. However, when laying a grassed area the type of grass must be appropriate to the intended recreational use. Meadow Grass was used on part of the SHEEPWASH site and provides a transition between the manicured landscape of the entrance area and the meadows within the proposed urban park.

Where passive recreation is proposed the provision of a more varied landscape is usually appropriate. This variety can be expressed in terms of plant colouring, textures and height. The use of semi-mature trees has been particularly successful when set within massed shrubs and vegetation (for example, CANNON STREET PARK and BROUGHTON HIGH AND ASCENSION). The use of unusual species such as bamboo, for example, in HACKNEY GROVE GARDEN, provides interest as well as presenting an attractive environment in which to sit or play.

The merits of different kinds of 'hard' landscaping

Like 'soft' landscaping it is appropriate that the 'hard' landscaping employed should reflect both the usage requirements and the traditions of the areas in which they are set.

Paths and paving are the central features of many environmental improvement projects. They need to follow 'desire lines', which can be subtly altered with mounding and planting. They need to be sufficiently robust to withstand the types of use envisaged (and that which may not be intended: cycling, motor cycling, go-karts, etc), but should not be over specified. They should at once be clear and visually unobtrusive. Projects that make good use of desire lines and that are constructed to withstand heavy usage include HATFIELD ROAD, TOWN CENTRE PARK and CANNON STREET PARK. Paths have also been used to enhance and provide access to natural features in projects such as the DERWENTHAUGH RIVERSIDE PARK. Also where appropriate the paving should blend in or complement the surroundings. This is successfully achieved in BEXLEY SQUARE where the use of paving bricks complements the Victorian brick built buildings that surround it.

Street or Park Furniture is very important, particularly the location, material and durability of seating. NOBLE'S QUAY/FISH QUAY has well sited seats which are welcoming and provide interesting visual outlooks and meeting places. Wood has proved the most durable material and few of the metal and concrete seats used in projects either look good or last well. Other furniture can make a major difference to the attractiveness and usefulness of the improvements. Simple things like litter bins work, if provided in adequate numbers and emptied. Railings can provide security, enhance the improvement works and reflect the character of nearby buildings and structures of interest, (for example, HACKNEY GROVE GARDEN), but they do require to be safe. Gates and fences can, by clearly delineating the site, give the impression of privacy and shelter. In some cases, railings and fencing may not be desirable if the objective is, as it is in Bolton, to make areas of public open space less traditional and formal.

Furniture should also take into account the surroundings of the area. In BEXLEY SQUARE for example, lamp posts, seats and bollards have been designed to complement the surrounding conservation area.

Walls can complement both formal and more informal 'soft' landscapes, providing an attractive addition to both texture and colour. They provide the opportunity for murals (HACKNEY GROVE GARDEN), and can create different levels to produce a more visually exciting landscape. The raised beds at TRENCHERFIELD MILL are good examples of the use of this technique and the retained walls at EXCHANGE STATION provide variety and interest.

Lighting can be helpful. To be fully successful an improvement can contribute to environmental quality at night as well as during daylight hours. Some projects need this, regular pathways can be made more secure by avoiding dark areas and sharp corners and through discreet 'street lighting'. Other projects can, through coloured lights, provide excitement and visual interest to passers by or, as at BEXLEY SQUARE, help meet conservation objectives. It has to be recognised however, that the provision of lighting can be very costly and although it may be desirable, it may not always be 'good value'.

Detailing is of great importance, particularly for well used, small sites, but even in more expansive and low cost schemes a poor entrance area, inadequate seating and facilities can seriously distract from the visual impact and enjoyment of the site. In community projects, providing scope for individuals and volunteers to 'leave their mark' can add interest and variety.

However, perhaps the most serious aspect of detailing is safety and great care is necessary to ensure that potentially dangerous materials, corners and protrusions are avoided.

Combining landscapes and activities

The needs of different individuals and groups are diverse and need to be successfully combined, as has been achieved in many of the projects. At BAYLIS ROAD, HATFIELD ROAD and the BANSTEADS the design and layout of the scheme has helped achieve this. In POTTERNEWTON PARK, the small children's play area benefits from being physically separated from areas more suitable for teenagers. Kickabout areas can provide for a variety of sports, and where managed, can cater for a wider range of user groups (for example BROUGHTON HIGH AND ASCENSION). However, difficulties can arise where 'desire lines' conflict with the needs of organised recreation.

Making the most of opportunities and changes

A feature common to many of the projects in this report is that they have capitalised on the opportunities presented by the landscape, built fabric and other resources in the vicinity.

The riverside site at NOBLE'S QUAY and coastal site of HENDON CLIFF TOP have both exploited the tremendous outlook and topography of the sites. Water has also played its part in the success of TRENCHERFIELD MILL and the DERWENTHAUGH RIVERSIDE PARK. Indeed, these projects illustrate the tremendous scope that exists, particularly within older industrial areas, to use waterways as a focus for improvement and to help reverse the development habits of several centuries that have so degraded rivers and canals.

A carefully planned landscape can, with the changes of the seasons, bring variety and interest to any landscaping project. This has been enhanced in a number of the case studies through the inventive planting of shrubs and flowers and mixtures of evergreen and deciduous species. For example, the planting of bulbs into the grass of TOWN CENTRE PARK, and the planting of herbaceous borders at TRENCHERFIELD MILL.

Just as important as seasonal changes in the visual environment are changes in recreational needs. Account has been taken of popular activities that require special facilities such as BMX bikes and experience has shown that meeting such needs need be neither costly, nor need it preclude later changes. One project that has been particularly successful in adapting to change is WINDMILL HILL CITY FARM, which has recently developed raised gardens for disabled and elderly gardeners, whilst herb and butterfly gardens are currently under construction.

Re-use of materials

Materials resulting from the clearance or tidying of a site can be put to imaginative use. Good use has been made of re-used materials in POTTERNEWTON PARK and especially at HACKNEY GROVE GARDEN where materials such as masonry faces and a local gravestone have been used to link the site to the surrounding area. In GREEN'S GARDENS and TRENCHERFIELD MILL artefacts have also helped to provide features and reference to the site history and surroundings.

Key conclusions

(i) Both 'natural' and 'manicured' design approaches work and are not necessarily exclusive options. Both will require management. Local opinion should be taken into account in deciding upon the approach.

(ii) Planting regimes have successfully provided interesting and varied environments throughout the seasons.

(iii) Visual benefit is subjective, it depends a great deal on the context and what was there before. Even very modest improvements, that are low cost and can be implemented quickly, are valued. However, in order to effect more fundamental changes in attitudes and behaviour, more substantial and costly improvements may be necessary.

(iv) Planting more mature trees can be best in visual and maintenance terms, but their expense requires that they are only used sparingly.

(v) The preferences, behaviour and needs of those living and working in the vicinity of the projects will change, so designs should be adaptable.

(vi) Detailing, particularly detailing concerning safety, security and maintenance, is critical.

4   Getting the most from limited resources

The question of what is 'cost effective' can be viewed from a number of different perspectives. There are a wide variety of rationales and objectives that have underpinned the improvements discussed in this report. The most frequent are:

- The improvement of facilities for recreation and leisure.

- The encouragement of private sector investment.

- The creation of new attractions within urban areas.

- The improvement of the quality of life for households.

Environmental improvements have also been undertaken to create and preserve the natural environment from an ecological viewpoint and to generate jobs and training opportunities.

Given such a wide range of objectives simple measures of 'cost effectiveness' and 'value for money', such as costs per unit of land improved and cost per household or user benefiting, may, if considered in isolation be inappropriate and misleading. Indeed, the 'good practice' · projects described in this report illustrate that costs per unit of land can, quite appropriately, vary very markedly, (see figure 3). Also, it is extremely difficult to establish definite and causal links between the improvements made and changes in the behaviour of businesses and householders so as to measure whether or not, and by how much, the objectives set have been achieved.

However, since resources are limited, projects need to be cost effective. It is considered that all of the projects discussed in this report have achieved this and could not have achieved the same ends at significantly lower cost.

There are a number of salient issues, discussed below, that affect cost effectiveness:

(a) the intensity of use relative to the quality of improvements;

(b) accounting for aftercare;

(c) the use of community and private sector resources.

The intensity of use relative to the quality of improvements

The intensity of improvement activity as measured in terms of cost per unit of land has varied enormously amongst the case studies. In each case the intensity has been appropriate to the objectives of the improvement and commensurate with the achievements. There are, however, dangers in undertaking work to either too low a standard or in overspecifying improvement works.

Low standard schemes can quickly revert to their former state and, by not crossing a minimum threshold, little, if any impact will be achieved. Over specification can be both expensive and can serve to undermine the confidence and commitment of those that are sceptical of the cost effectiveness of urban environmental improvements. Careful consideration is necessary at the planning stage in order to ensure that the site's specification is appropriate given its context and potential for use. This is especially so for projects that have involved derelict land reclamation and improvements to the built fabric.

This report has been mainly concerned with environmental improvements and enhancements to sites, but several of the projects described have involved derelict land reclamation (for example, BROUGHTON HIGH AND ASCENSION and HENDON CLIFF TOP). In these projects the costs and standards of reclamation have been suitable for the after use envisaged. However, difficulties and costs may arise on such sites because of unforseen problems such as contamination, drainage or sub-surface structures. In order to avoid problems at a later stage, it is sensible to carry out initial site tests before finalising a scheme – if finance and time are available.

Figure 3: Relative costs of improvement works

Category	Project	Costs of Improvement
Public Open Space for Passive Leisure Use and Walkways	Town Centre Park	••••
	Hendon Cliff Top	•
	Sheepwash	•
Active and Organised Recreation Projects	Hatfield Road	••
	Cannon Street Park	••
	Potternewton Park	••
Housing Related	Black Patch	Not Available[1]
	Green's Gardens	••••
	Hylton Dene	•
	Broughton High and Ascension	••••
	Banstead	•••
Visual Enhancements	Exchange Station Car Park	•••
	Baylis Road	•••••
	Nobles Quay/Fish Quay	•••••
Projects In Industrial and Commercial Areas	Derwenthaugh Riverside Park	Not Available[1]
	Trencherfield Mill	•••
	Electric Avenue	••••
	Bexley Square	•••••
Voluntary Sector Projects	Lever Edge	•••
	Hackney Grove Garden	•••••
	Windmill Hill City Farm	••

Key: Costs of Improvement Works (Per Square Metre)

•   less than £2
••   £2 to £5
•••   £5 to £10
•••• £10 to £25
••••• more than £25

[1] It has not been possible to reliably estimate the costs per square metre of improvements at Black Patch or Derwenthaugh Riverside Park because of the particularly complex layout of improvements works.

Comparatively small sites and buildings, not necessarily of much environmental significance, can consume very large levels of resources, whilst, at the same time, relatively low cost improvements on other sites (such as HENDON CLIFF TOP and HYLTON DENE) where conditions were particularly poor before improvement can make a major contribution to the environment.

An estimate of the number of people that will benefit and assessments of the amount of benefit that they will gain should be considered when assessing the potential cost effectiveness of alternative projects. HACKNEY GROVE GARDEN, for example, is a small site which has received a high intensity of resources, yet is

cost effective because of the high intensity of use which it attracts.

As far as improvements for active recreation are concerned, the surfaces and facilities need to be of adequate quality. Improvements to a playing surface can greatly increase the usage of a facility as illustrated by POTTERNEWTON PARK. Providing a high quality surface can also have additional advantages such as requiring less maintenance and/or being less susceptible to waterlogging. BROUGHTON HIGH and ASCENSION and BAYLIS ROAD both provide examples where high quality surfaces have been sensibly chosen.

Accounting for aftercare

Whatever the nature of the improvements there will be costs associated with maintaining them. Section 2 of the report has discussed factors that can reduce these costs and improve management. The maintenance costs cannot, however, be eliminated.

Unfortunately, problems have arisen because, given the present arrangements for funding, it is often easier to acquire resources for the initial improvement works than for continuing maintenance. This applies both to finance, where emphasis has been given to capital rather than revenue spending at central government level, and to inputs from volunteers and MSC labour. There is a perhaps natural preference for volunteers to work on interesting improvement works rather than routine chores and maintenance, and aftercare work provides less opportunities for training suitable for MSC programmes.

One consequence of this is that aftercare and maintenance of environmental improvements has often become the responsibility of existing parks and recreation departments. However, they have not usually has their funding increased to match the additional workload and often do not have the expertise for managing anything other than traditional urban parks. Thus, in some instances aftercare has been inadequate and the improvements have deteriorated.

What is required for each improvement is, as discussed in Section 2, the preparation and costing of a management plan *at the planning stage*. This could usefully be complimented with a more flexible attitude on behalf of central government towards revenue spending, either through providing additional revenue resources or through allowing capital resources to be used for maintenance purposes. More generally, environmental improvements should be preceded by a 'cost-in-use' exercise, taking account of the anticipated 'life' of the improvements, the maintenance requirements, costs and management during its life cycle, and trade-offs between initial specification and aftercare needs. Such exercises will, through helping ensure the durability of improvements, improve cost effectiveness.

Using community and private sector resources

One important aspect of cost-effectiveness is the extent to which improvements directly draw in community and private sector resources. One measure of this is the ratio of public to non-public resources or 'leverage'.

The extent of private sector leverage has been low in the projects discussed in this report. However, if this criterion of cost-effectiveness is applied, projects are likely to be more successful if they are undertaken in areas where there is more private sector interest and where the projects are, at least in part, of direct benefit to private sector operators. ELECTRIC AVENUE and BEXLEY SQUARE provide examples of improvements that meet both these conditions.

The encouragement of private sector investment is, however, an ambitious objective. It is likely to require a high standard of improvement, sufficient to transform the image of the area. Often this can only be achieved if a substantial number of environmental problems are tackled as part of a concerted effort. In a sense there exists a threshold which must be breached if improvements are to help meet this objective.

Drawing visitors and tourists to urban areas is becoming an increasing important objective of environmental improvements and related developments. However, the creation or enhancement of attractions within urban areas again requires high quality improvements that are both visually striking and well maintained.

The extent of leverage of other community resources has been higher in the projects reviewed. Leverage of this type has been achieved where the projects have responded to local needs, been imaginative in scope and been organised and implemented with energy and commitment. The lead for these projects has come from either the community itself (for example, HACKNEY GROVE GARDEN) or the local authority, (for example, GREEN'S GARDENS).

In order to maximise the improvement to the quality of life of householders in urban areas the design of a project must conform to the priorities of the local community. Both high and low quality improvements may be effective, but both need to be set within programmes of improvement that demonstrate a fundamental commitment to urban environmental improvement.

Key conclusions

(i)   Resources should not be spread too thinly. There is a minimum threshold below which improvements will have little or no impact.

(ii)   Aftercare and maintenance needs to be considered at the planning stage. Successful projects require revenue resources.

(iii) Community and private sector resources can and should be drawn into environmental improvement projects. This can both improve the cost effectiveness of public sector expenditure and help generate commitment to the improvements.

(iv)   Improvements should be to a specification commensurate with the benefits that can be derived. Those schemes which will clearly consume high levels of resources with few benefits are to be avoided.

(v)   The physical quality of cost effective improvements will vary according to the objectives set for the improvement works.

5 Learning by doing

This final section of the synthesis discusses approaches to the monitoring and assessment of urban environmental improvements. There are several reasons why monitoring is important:

- Monitoring provides feedback on the achievements of projects and the extent to which objectives set are being met.

- Feedback from monitoring and assessment can inform policy and priorities. This is relevant to both strategic and project specific policy issues concerning design, management and maintenance.

- During the implementation of improvement works close attention needs to be paid to physical progress and financial control.

- Regular inspections of improved sites are necessary to identify needs for repair and maintenance.

By and large, and as described in more detail in the evaluation of environmental projects funded under the Urban Programme (Department of the Environment, 1986) there has been little formal monitoring and assessment of the achievements of urban environmental projects. The main exceptions to this are where revenue projects have been closely assessed as part of a formal funding review procedure.

Urban environmental improvements pursue a very wide range of objectives, often including recreational, social, economic and housing as well as physical aims. The local circumstances and base line physical conditions within which environmental projects have been undertaken vary widely. These factors make it difficult to assess the performance of projects and to make direct comparisons between projects developed in different contexts.

Nevertheless, there are four areas, discussed below, in which monitoring and assessment practice could be improved:

(i) Clearly specifying objectives.

(ii) Setting improvements within 'action programmes'.

(iii) Developing output measures for programmes of improvement work.

(iv) Improving feedback from users and beneficiaries.

Specifying objectives

There is usually scope for improving the definition and specification of most environmental improvement objectives. Where possible objectives should be set in such a way that their achievement (or otherwise) can be assessed after the improvements have been undertaken and set against the costs of improvement work.

Setting improvements within an 'action programme'

Where appropriate, individual environmental projects should be undertaken within the context of clearly defined physical planning, housing and improvement proposals for the areas in which they are set. The form of these proposals will vary and could best be described as an 'Action Programme'. They would form a clearly understood measure against which progress can be assessed and, as discussed in Section 2, help in generating commitment and enthusiasm towards the improvements for those directly involved and likely to benefit.

Output measures for programmes of improvement work

Many of the projects described in this report are examples of approaches that have been implemented on a programmed basis within the districts concerned. Straightforward output measures may be appropriate to indicate the progress and aggregate achievements of these programmes. Whilst great care will be required in their interpretation, output measures may be particularly relevant to environmental projects involving recreation objectives.

Output measures concering urban environmental improvements will be particularly relevant when set against the scale of the problems that are being addressed. In general, with the notable exception of the problem of derelict land which was surveyed in 1974 and 1982, little is known of the scale of the environmental problems that have been addressed by the projects. Various surveys have been undertaken of problems, such as limited open space, 'untidy' land and the obsolete and disused built fabric, but, in general, these have not been part of a regular process to monitor urban environmental conditions and the progress of improvements.

Improved monitoring of this type could help inform priorities and could provide the basis for improved resource allocation decisions at central and local government levels.

Feedback from users and beneficiaries

A critical aspect of successful projects has been their responsiveness to local needs and priorities. At the project planning stage it is important to involve and consult with those living and working in the area. There are ways of involving the community in implementing projects (see Section 1) and there is also great scope for taking account of the views of users and beneficiaries in the monitoring process. However, this is uncommon despite there being several important reasons for this activity.

Firstly, almost all projects are undertaken to directly or indirectly meet the needs of those living in the vicinity of the improvements. Secondly, the needs of a community are continually changing and improvements need to be responsive to these. Thirdly, needs of different groups within the community are very varied and deliberate and systematic effort is necessary to establish whether the needs of different groups, some of whom will not be very vocal, are being met.

In the study of environmental projects funded under the Urban Programme (Department of the Environment, 1986) the consultants talked to over 800 individuals and businesses living and working in the vicinity of environmental projects or making use of them. Their views and comments have informed the findings of this report. None of them had, with the exception of residents at BLACK PATCH, previously been asked about the benefits they had received from the projects.

Key conclusions

(i)   The level of monitoring should be commensurate with the needs of maintenance/aftercare and the needs to inform future policy.

(ii) Feedback should include evidence from those that are meant to have benefited.

(iii) Monitoring should be undertaken of progress compared with explicit objectives and targets.

(iv) The aggregate achievements of environmental improvements should be set against measures of the scale of the problems that they address.

Case Study 1: Town Centre Park, Sunderland; The view across the green to the church, almshouses and leisure centre

Case Study 2: Hendon Cliff Top, Sunderland; The newly landscaped clifftops provide a valuable addition to scarce amenity open space

Case Study 3: Sheepwash Urban Park, Sandwell; The first phase involved the provision of entrances and access to the park which is now under planting

Case Study 4: Hatfield Road, Bolton; The provision of play areas and seating for local residents was a feature of the refurbishment of the Victorian park

Case Study 5: Cannon Street Park, Bolton; A new park created to provide a grassed area

Case Study 6: Greens Gardens, Nottingham; Residents with young children benefit from the play area, in an area that was previously lacking adequate facilities

Case Study 7: Potternewton Park, Leeds; A traditional Victorian park improved with new facilities provided for ball games

Case Study 8: Black Patch Estate, Sandwell; An aerial view of the extensive improvements made to this cut-off estate

Case Study 9: Hylton Dene, Sunderland; A scheme to improve access to, appearance and use of, an extensive area of poor quality open space and woodland

Case Study 10: Broughton High and Ascension, Salford; The reclamation of a housing clearance area to provide new public open space and play areas

Case Study 11: The Bansteads, Leeds; The provision of two play areas, seating areas, a school garden and other facilities made possible by derelict housing clearance

Case Study 12: The Exchange Station Car Park, Bradford; Peripheral landscaping of a centrally situated development site and provision of a temporary car park

Case Study 13: Baylis Road, Lambeth; A new public open space created on a former coach and car park

Case Study 14: Nobles Quay/Fish Quay, Sunderland; An operational and environmental improvement of the quays and subsequent development as public open space for dockers and local residents

Case Study 15: Derwenthaugh Riverside Park, Gateshead; Improvement and construction of landscaped pathways as part of an Industrial Improvement Area

Case Study 16: Trencherfield Mill, Wigan; Peripheral landscaping of a car park and a derelict piece of land next to a prestigous tourist facility

Case Study 17: Electric Avenue, Lambeth; Refurbishment of a run down shopping street in central Brixton

Case Study 18: Bexley Square, Salford; Pedestrianisation of part of a square in a Conservation Area adjacent to a major route into Salford

Case Study 19: Lever Edge, Bolton; A voluntary sector project to provide safer access to a school for local children

Case Study 20: Hackney Grove Garden, Hackney; The derelict, sunken site of a burnt-out toy factory converted into a community garden

Case Study 21: Windmill Hill City Farm, Bristol; A former scrap yard transformed into a city farm, a garden and thriving community facility

Part III

CASE STUDIES

Introduction

The individual case studies referred to in Part II are now presented. Each is preceded by a summary which indicates the basic details of the scheme and highlights aspects of good practice. Colour pictures of each scheme are included in between Parts II and III of this volume.

The case studies have been grouped in six categories.

- Public open space for passive leisure use and walkways

- Active and organised recreation projects

- Housing related improvements

- Visual enhancements

- Projects in industrial and commercial areas

- Voluntary sector projects.

Public open space for passive leisure use and walkways

1   Town Centre Park, Sunderland

Design features

- Strong visual image
- Footpath layout to ease pedestrian movement
- Provision of flowerbeds and planting in traditional style

Beneficiaries

- Pedestrians
- Nearby shops
- Residents of almshouses
- Churchgoers
- Leisure centre users

Good practice

- Public consultation
- Retention and enhancement of existing features
- Beneficial to local traders
- Formed part of long term strategy
- Successful planting regimes
- Combines functional improvements for pedestrians, with visual improvement
- Relatively low maintenance requirements
- Major visual improvement achieved
- Meets environmental and economic objectives.

Key facts

The creation of a formal park with paved walkways, grassed areas and flowerbeds on housing clearance land in the town centre.

Size:		9,000 square metres
Costs:	*Capital:*	£111,000 (1979–83)
	Revenue:	Estimated cost of maintenance required per annum £2,000. Actual revenue expenditure on maintenance 1985/6 £824
Funding sources:		Urban Programme (capital) Borough of Sunderland (revenue)
Initiator:		Planning Department, Borough of Sunderland
Implementation:		Planning Department, Borough of Sunderland, Works Department, Borough of Sunderland

This is a town park in the traditional sense: 0.9 hectares of paved walkways, grass and flower beds in the centre of Sunderland. On a site that was first used for housing, and then for car parking (figure 1), trees and shrubs now provide colour all year, and an historic grassy area, known locally as 'the Green', has been successfully retained. Lying close to the city's main shopping and market areas, this attractive park has become popular and busy. Visually, it reduces the dominance of a nearby leisure centre and complements the buildings of an adjoining conservation area.

Origins

Sunderland's Borough Planning Department see the town park as part of a longer term strategy which has two elements: environmental improvement of prominent sites and the encouragement of commercial confidence in the city centre. As early as 1974, a report to the Director of Planning emphasised the importance of the proposed town park in enhancing the adjoining conservation area. By improving this unsightly former housing site – increasingly a focus for flytipping – it was thought that the commercial interest in nearby shops could be retained.

The park became one of a series of environmental improvements in the neighbourhood. The stone-cleaning of St Michael's Church, some nearby

Figure 1: Prior to improvements the site was taken up by car parks and a cut-off circular green

almshouses and a number of public and privately owned buildings within the conservation area, all took place under the Department of the Environment's Special Environmental Assistance Scheme. More recently, other buildings adjacent to the site of the proposed park, but outside the conservation area, were tackled during Operation Clean-Up in 1979. A landscape design of the proposed park was prepared for detailed consideration in the same year. As part of

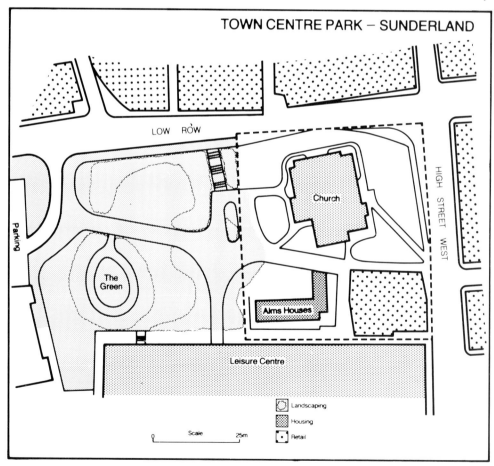

Plan 1: Town Centre Park, Sunderland

this process the general public were invited to comment on the proposals at a series of displays in the centre of Sunderland.

Design, Implementation and Maintenance

'The Green' has been kept as a prominent feature of the park, with a paved perimeter walkway surrounded by herbaceous borders and hedegrows (see colour photograph). The oval shape of 'The Green' is echoed elsewhere in the park in a second, small feature which forms an attractive focus at the crossing of the main walkways. This comprises a series of levels: first a rockery, then grass planted with different kinds of crocus, followed by layers of bedding plants and shrubs. Five heavy standard trees (mountain and manna ash) form the top level.

Many varieties of shrub and tree have been planted around the perimeter of the park and adjacent to its walkways, partially screening the leisure centre. The rotation of bedding plants, the use of hybrid tea roses and old favourites such as hydrangea, all provide the park with a traditional image. Seasonal colour is provided by red and pink flowering rhododendron, pink-blossoming oramental cherry and white flowering manna ash. The planting regime has been relatively successful with few natural losses occurring.

High quality paving – red and marigold concrete blocks – is a notable feature of the park, serving as pedestrian routes between car parks, the leisure centre and nearby shops. The quality of the paving serves to provide visual impact and also to ensure durability in the face of heavy pedestrian usage. Steps and retaining walls complement the paving which shows a good understanding of the directional requirements of pedestrians (figure 2).

In December 1979, using funds made available under Operation Clean-Up, work started on the park with the removal of flytipped rubbish and debris left

Figure 2: Pedestrians access has been eased and the outlook improved for the almshouses and church

from construction of the leisure centre. Using Urban Programme resources work continued until April 1983 when the project was completed, as programmed. Subsequently a small sum was allocated for a flower bed and bollards to deter car drivers from parking on the paved areas.

Project schedule – Town Centre Park

February 1974	A report by the Director of Planning 'Conservation in Sunderland, Bishopwearmouth' recommended the establishment of a Town Park
1979	Scheme included within approved IAP submission. Detailed drawings prepared.
December 1979	Preparatory works undertaken during Operation Clean Up.
January 1980	Project works began
March 1983	Project works completed
Spring 1983	Bollards and flower bed placed to stop motorists from driving onto the park

Cost

The scheme was implemented by the Works Department of the Borough of Sunderland at a total capital cost of £111,000. Revenue requirements to maintain the scheme are estimated by the Borough of Sunderland to be £2,000 per annum. Expenditure on maintenance in the year to April 1986 was, however, only £824.

Beneficiaries

All the year round, pedestrians make heavy use of the park's walkways as through routes from the nearby car parks and shops to the leisure centre, bus station and main shopping areas.

The park has been of particular benefit to those attending St Michael's Church and to the residents of the almshouses for, in both cases, access has been eased and the outlook dramatically improved. In the summer months, the park is well used for casual recreation particularly at lunchtimes when students from the nearby polytechnic and townspeople alike take full advantage of its green spaces.

The visual environment for shops overlooking the park and those within the conservation area has certainly changed. Shop owners have welcomed the Borough's efforts, although they feel that tangible, commercial benefits are yet to come.

Overall the response to this project has been especially good, with everyone interviewed agreeing that a considerable visual enhancement has been secured. Residents thought the park was 'lovely all year round' and appreciated the sensitive blending of materials and the traditional style. 'It seems', one said, that the park has always been here'.

The comparatively low cost of the formal high quality treatment of this central location is clearly appropriate and commensurate with the benefits derived by people living and working in Sunderland.

2   Hendon Cliff Top, Sunderland

Design features

- Soft landscaping works to enhance site

- Provision of car parking spaces

- Improved access routes to the site and the seawall

- Basic drainage works in parts in the site

Beneficiaries

- Local residents

- Anglers using the seawall

Good practice

- Public consultation

- Effective use of coastal site

- Low maintenance requirements

- Has met needs for open space and objective to improve the local environment.

Key facts

Reclamation works to a former coastal dumping ground and notorious eyesore using a Derelict Land Grant. These basic works were enhanced through general landscaping and the construction of a car park using Urban Programme resources.

Size:		80,000 square metres
Cost:	Capital:	£127,800
	Revenue:	Estimated annual expenditure on maintenance £2,000.
Funding sources:		Urban Programme (£52,800) (capital) Derelict Land Grant (£70,000) Borough of Sunderland (£5,000 + revenue)
Initiator:		Planning Department, Borough of Sunderland
Implementation:		Direct Labour Organisation, Borough of Sunderland

Coastal sites have a high potential amenity value for leisure and recreation, particularly when close to centres of population. The reclamation of the cliff top at Hendon, in Sunderland, has transformed a notorious eyesore and dangerous dumping ground (figure 3) into an area of coastal open space. Subsequent low cost enhancement works have made a valuable addition to scarce amenity open space.

Figure 3: The dangerous waste dumping ground that was Hendon Cliff Top

Origins

Industrial dereliction in Sunderland is considerable both in scale and in number of sites requiring treatment. Coastal Hendon, hemmed between a paper factory, gas works and the sea, was becoming increasingly dangerous. Although access was restricted indiscriminate dumping of waste materials had taken place over a number of years. In addition tidal erosion was undermining the cliffs. In spite of these dangers residents from the nearby housing areas were venturing onto the cliff top for there was little open space of any kind in the Hendon area. Indeed, a Borough of Sunderland report entitled 'Open Space Recreation' recognised Hendon as an inner area with a 'severe shortage' of amenity open space.

For these reasons, Hendon Cliff Top became a priority within the derelict land reclamation programme of the Borough of Sunderland Planning Department and a Derelict Land Grant aided scheme was undertaken to remove the worst dereliction and dumped materials. However, it was clear that land adjoining the reclamation site would require upgrading if this part of the coast was to be fully restored. An enhancement scheme, using Urban Programme funds, was subsequently proposed, soon after reclamation works were completed in 1981, and plans were drawn up taking into account local residents' opinions.

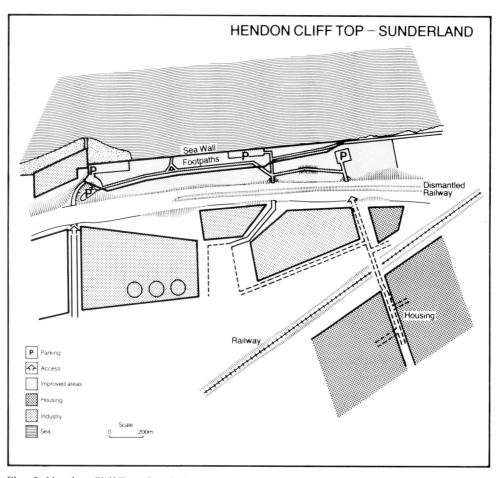

Plan 2: Hendon Cliff Top, Sunderland

Design, Implementation and Maintenance

Elaborate design is not a feature of the Hendon Cliff Top scheme. Rather emphasis has been placed upon bringing a former derelict and dangerous site back into recreational use with footpaths and track access to the site together with car parking (figure 4). Indeed, a more elaborate design would have been inappropriate in such an exposed coastal location. Considering the harsh climatic conditions, the size of the site (8ha) and the appalling conditions that existed prior to improvement, a substantial transformation has taken place, making a cost effective use of available resources.

The Borough Planning Department readily agree that there are additional improvements that may still be made. These would raise the quality of the improvement works but at a cost (it is suggested) not commensurate with the additional benefits derived. Within the context of limited resources and large scale problems, the greater proportion of benefit has been derived from basic improvements. Indeed, the scheme has achieved a particularly 'natural' feel at relatively low cost.

These basic improvement works, which began in February 1983, involved the regrading, soiling and seeding of the area adjoining the reclamation site, some standard tree planting and fencing. Basic drainage works were implemented over parts of the site. Access was significantly improved by laying dolomite footpaths and roadways. Two prominent car parks, each adjacent to the seawall, were provided to accommodate car users.

Private contractors and the Public Works Department of the Borough of Sunderland undertook the works. These were implemented and completed as programmed in January 1984.

Figure 4: Access has been improved by footpaths and roadways. Car parking is adjacent to the sea walls

Project schedule – Hendon Cliff Top

1980/81	Reclamation undertaken using Derelict Land Grant
1981	Proposals put forward for enhancement works and plans drawn up.
1981	Project included in approved IAP submission for 1982/3 and 1983/4.
February 1983	Enhancement works began.
January 1984	Enhancement works completed.

Cost

The costs of the reclamation and enhancement works were £75,800 and £52,800 respectively. Derelict Land Grant accounted for £70,000 of the reclamation monies whilst £5,000 was derived from the Borough of Sunderland's main programme budgets. The enhancement works were funded solely from Urban Programme resources in 1982/83 and 1983/84. Revenue expenditure on necessary maintenance has been estimated at £2,000 by the Borough of Sunderland. However, vandalism has been a particular problem of this site and the maintenance estimate does not include the cost of replacement planting.

Beneficiaries

This cliff top scheme provides a significant addition to the scarce amenity open space in Hendon which has benefited the city as a whole. People now travel to the site from all over Sunderland, especially on summer weekends. Improved access and car parking has encouraged use of the sea wall by anglers and promenaders alike.

Residents of Hendon who were questioned felt that the area was now much more pleasant to live in and several pointed out that the improvement works had encouraged them to stay in the area. However, ease of access and the openness of the site makes it prone to use by youths riding trailbikes, which has been a cause for complaint. Nevertheless, all those users spoken to who had used the site before improvement now used it more often and were unanimous that the removal of dumped materials constituted an outstanding visual improvement.

3   Sheepwash, Sandwell

Design features

- Gravel pathways and high quality fencing and gateway as part of the entrance
- Mix of bushes and trees
- Combination of 'manicured' and 'natural' landscaping styles.

Beneficiaries

- Local residents
- Schoolchildren

Good practice

- Public consultation
- Forms integral part of a larger project as well as part of a district wide environmental improvement programme
- Involvement of local school
- Successful planting regime
- Low maintenance requirements
- Helped develop voluntary sector interest.

Key facts

The first phase of the creation of an urban park in Sandwell. The project forms one of the entrances to the park (currently being developed) and has involved the landscaping of what was once a derelict site.

Size:	10,000 square metres
Cost: Capital:	£18,500 1983–84
Revenue:	Not estimated on project basis.
Funding sources:	Urban Programme (capital) Sandwell MBC (revenue)
Initiator:	Technical Services Department and Recreation Amenities Department, Sandwell MBC
Implementation:	Recreation and Amenities Department and Technical Services Department, Sandwell MBC. Local schoolchildren involved in planting.

The Sheepwash Project is an ambitious programme of work being undertaken over a number of years to create an urban park and woodland area on a derelict 28 hectare site in Sandwell. A small part (1 ha) of the site adjacent to Dunkirk Avenue was selected for treatment under Sandwell Metropolitan Borough Council's Environmental Improvement Programme. This programme was set up to landscape and improve individual sites. The Dunkirk Avenue site illustrates a number of aspects of good practice.

The site has been designed to be an improvement in its own right but at the same time it is complementary to the urban park project. Dereliction and flytipping have been removed from proximity to housing and the local school has benefited from an involvement in the development of the project. Finally, the site is a good example of what has been achieved in Sandwell's Environmental Improvement Programme under which numerous sites in the borough have been improved over the last few years.

Origins

Located in the Great Bridge area of Sandwell the land known locally as Sheepwash is a partially reclaimed tract of land formerly used for mineral extraction and more recently for tipping. Sheepwash is bounded by the Birmingham to Wolverhampton railway line which is itself the subject of environmental improvement through the Greenline Project, an initiative involving local authorities, British Rail and British Waterways Board and large areas of predominantly public sector housing.

The overall plan for Sheepwash is an ambitious programme of work to create an urban park with an emphasis on developing and conserving natural habitats. Work on the park has started but is seen as a long term project. At the same time Sandwell's Technical Services and Recreation and Amenities departments have developed an Environmental Improvement Programme (EIP) to address particular site problems throughout the borough. A small part of Sheepwash, approximately one hectare, situated on Dunkirk Avenue was selected for treatment under the EIP because of its poor appearance, the presence of flytipping, and because of its proximity to housing and the Newtown Primary School.

The work on this site was designed to be an environmental improvement in its own right, but at the same time enhancing land that would provide one of the main entrances to the urban park.

Two different styles of landscaping have been employed on either side of the boundary fence. On the side that fronts Dunkirk Avenue and is closest to the housing area the emphasis is on a neat formal landscape which comprises a grassed area with the plant-

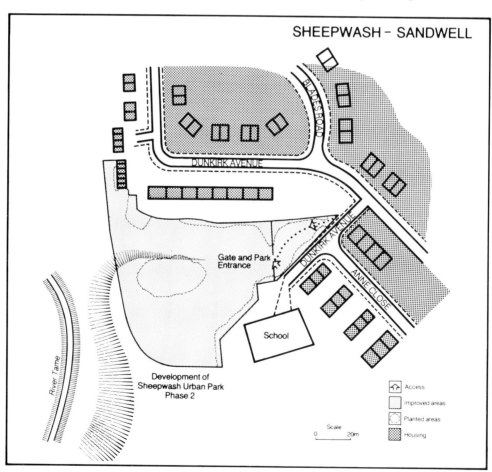

Plan 3: Sheepwash Urban Park, Sandwell

Figure 5: The boundary of the site has been planted, with footpaths leading through to the park entrance

ing of native bushes, whips and semi-mature trees. Most of the planting has taken place on the margins of the site which have been slightly mounded to provide a barrier between the site and the road (Dunkirk Avenue). This barrier has been completed by the construction of a low wooden fence (figure 5).

On the other side of the boundary fence is the part of the site which forms part of Sheepwash Urban Park. The design approach here is more informal and acts as a transition between the park entrance and the natural habitats planned for the Sheepwash site. Meadow grass has been used to give a natural effect. A wooden fence and planting acts as a barrier between the site and Newton Primary School. This part of the site also includes small blocks of dense planting and the construction of a gravel pathway into Sheepwash.

Work on the Dunkirk Avenue site has been undertaken, from the design to implementation stage, by Sandwell MBC's Recreation and Amenities Department under instruction from the Department of Technical Services. The work was undertaken between 1983 and 1984.

An integral part of the implementation stage was the involvement of Newtown Primary School. School children were heavily involved in the planting of trees and bushes and the school has subsequently used the development of the Sheepwash project as a basis for environmental studies.

The involvement of the school, together with the choice of native species and the positioning of the planted areas (away from footpaths and often protected by fencing), has reduced both natural losses and those due to vandalism. Maintenance is undertaken by the Recreation and Amenities Department, currently on an ongoing basis as the urban park is implemented.

Project schedule – Sheepwash

1978	Sandwell start Environmental Improvement Programme; public
	consultations held to decide future usage of Sheepwash
	Adoption of urban park plan.
1983	Expansion of Environmental Improvement Programme as Sandwell is awarded Programme Area status.
	Dunkirk Avenue site approved as an E.I.P. project.
1983–84	Work undertaken on Dunkirk Avenue site. Local primary school involved in planting.
1984	Reclamation work starts at Sheepwash. Ongoing construction of urban park envisaged into the 1990's.

Costs

The landscaping of the Dunkirk Avenue site was funded through Sandwell's Environmental Improvement Programme (EIP), at a cost of £18,500 in 1983/84. Although this cost is relatively high in comparison to other sites treated under the EIP it is accounted for by the high quality and the durability of the design which has the site's role as an entrance to the urban park in mind. By contrast many other schemes in the EIP are designed solely as visual improvements and do not have to cater for high levels of usage. The EIP is supported by the Urban Programme.

Beneficiaries

Residents in the locality of the scheme were almost unanimous in their support for the project. Some initial fears of vandalism and disturbance have not been realised and it was generally thought that the removal of a tipping area and the landscaping of the site represents a substantial improvement. There was particular enthusiasm for the expansion of the project to encompass the rest of the Sheepwash area. Those who have recently bought property – from Sandwell Housing Department – believe that the existing and proposed improvements can only be beneficial to property values. Local residents now make more use of the site, and its popularity is anticipated to increase when the urban park is completed. The siting of the footpath to avoid direct contact with the rear gardens of housing and the provision of fencing and trees as a screen on some parts of the site are particularly appreciated. The only sizeable disturbance mentioned by residents was the occasional use of the site and the proposed park area by motorcyclists (not a new activity here).

Newtown Primary School have been involved with the development of the site from the start. As part of the school's involvement with tree planting on the site

41

staff explored with children the historical development of the area. Children have been involved in monitoring the growth and care of trees and the colonisation of insects and other wildlife. They have been asked to think imaginatively about the further development of the Sheepwash Urban Park. The school's headmaster thinks that the project has been of immense value to the children, providing new experiences and a stimulus for educational work. He is anxious to maintain the school's involvement as the project develops (on the current site and in the urban park).

Further development
The original plan for Sheepwash dates back to 1978 when, after a series of public consultations and a consideration of a variety of options for the 28 hectare site, Sandwell's Technical Services Department made initial plans for the reclamation of the Sheepwash area with a view to create an urban park based on native species and with an emphasis on nature convervation.

Some features of the site, for example the series of pools, are to be retained partly for environmental reasons (to allow for planting of reeds and to act as a habitat for birds) and partly for practical reasons (the pools act as a hydraulic system for the nearby River Tame). Indeed a new pool has been added to aid the development of a wetland habitat.

The park is being slowly developed over a number of years. At present the emphasis is on land reclamation, the reduction or removal of toxicity in both soil and water, and also on the planting of blocks of shrubs and trees to act as focal points for the urban forest, providing areas of mature planting as the park develops. Pathways through the park are being created or improved.

The ambitious nature of the programme is reflected in the extensive consultations with wildlife and conservation groups and in the diverse sources of funding. Consultants and advisors have included the Urban Wildlife Group, the Forestry Commission, Royal Society for the Protection of Birds, the British Trust for Conservation Volunteers and the Nature Conservancy Council. Sources of funding have included the Urban Programme, Derelict Land Grant (the main source to date) and the Severn Trent Water Authority.

Whilst the park development has a series of objectives and priorities, future funding and time requirements are as yet unsure. The design of the park for the areas yet to be planted is currently being prepared prior to consultation.

In the near future Sandwell's Planning Department hope to have signs and information boards on the Dunkirk Avenue site and within the urban park. The Newton Primary School is proposed as a base for interpretative material. Some publicity and media coverage has occurred for the project although currently the local authority discourage extensive use of the site in its current partially derelict and dangerous state.

Whilst it is, as yet, too early to comment on the design, implementation and management of Sheepwash urban park there are already indications of good practice. The project is undeniably ambitious and of a scale to ensure both a wide range of beneficiaries and scope for experimentation. It is conservation minded and a move away from the normal treatment (substantial grassed areas) often associated with large derelict land sites. Also it has sought to use and to encourage a wide range of participation in terms of local groups, including the Sandwell Naturalists Trust, and national organisations. Finally, it is designed with a long term in mind.

Active and organised recreation projects

4   Hatfield Road, Bolton

Design features

- Extensive planting of trees and shrubs
- New and improved footpaths
- New tarmac play area.
- General landscaping works.

Beneficiaries

- Local residents

Good practice

- Responded to local needs for play facilities
- Improved upon an existing facility
- Part of a programme of works to reverse decline of parks and play areas
- Combines facilities for active and passive users

Key facts

Refurbishment of a run-down Victorian park in Bolton and provision of additional facilities.

Size:	5,000 square metres
Cost: Capital:	£19,000 1982–83
Revenue:	£4,500 per annum.
Funding sources:	Urban Programme (capital) Bolton MBC (revenue)
Initiator:	Department of Environmental Services, Bolton Metropolitan Borough Council.
Implementation:	Department of Environmental Services, Bolton Metropolitan Borough Council.

The Hatfield Road, park and playground, situated to the immediate north of central Bolton, is one of a series of such facilities selected by the Department of Environmental Services of Bolton Metropolitan Borough Council for upgrading and refurbishment. The work undertaken has improved the usage and benefits of existing facilities and particularly play facilities for local children of differing age groups. The improvements to the park are easily noticeable to local residents as the site is completely enclosed by housing.

Origins
The Parks and Recreation division of the Environmental Services Department, Bolton MBC, had drawn up a list of all existing play areas and playgrounds within the inner urban area of Bolton. Many were found to be in need of repair and refurbishment. As part of an overall strategy to increase and improve the provision of open space and play facilities the Parks and Recreation division looked at the areas of greatest need and the areas where the greatest opportunity existed to either create new parks (see CANNON STREET PARK, BOLTON) or refurbish old ones.

The Parks and Recreation division sought to improve all of their parks and sites in the inner urban area, but restrictions on resources led to a selection of parks, evenly spread through inner Bolton, for upgrading.

Six parks and play areas were chosen, all well established and all in some state of decline. Preparatory work by the Parks and Recreation division underlined the scale of work required to substantially improve the existing facilities. Whilst the costs of refurbishment were variable, dependent on size and the nature of the facilities, the average capital cost of refurbishing a park was in the region of £30,000. With an annual budget of approximately £50,000, (derived from the Urban Programme) allocated for the programme of refurbishment, improvements had to be phased over a period of time. One of the parks selected for improvement was located in Hatfield Road in an area of Victorian terracing, with high proportions of families with young children and elderly residents. The park, although small (0.5 ha), catered for a large and diverse number of users but play facilities were both ageing and limited and at the same time the overall appearance of the park was deteriorating making it a strong candidate for refurbishment.

Design, implementation and maintenance
For the most part the existing layout of the park has been retained. However, the intention of the refurbishment was to go further than general 'tidying

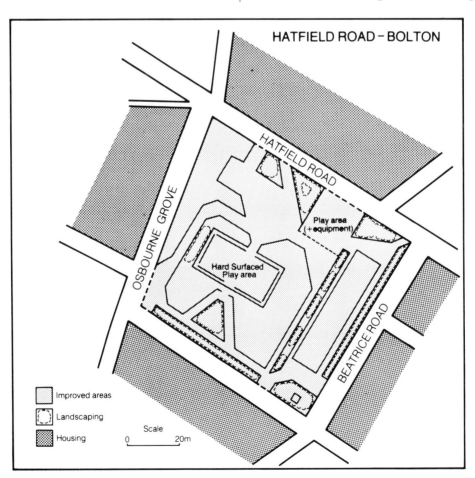

Plan 4: The refurbishment of Hatfield Road Park

Figure 6: New seating has been provided at the lower (Beatrice Road) end of the park

Figure 7: New planting includes a variety of trees and bushes

up' and maintenance work, and to make improvements to children's play facilities a high priority. This entailed new and more modern (in design) play equipment and a new walled tarmac play area for ball games which replaced a shale play area that had become littered with bricks and broken glass. The pathways in the park had deteriorated badly and had become untidy and in some cases almost overgrown. All pathways were cleared and tidied. Where necessary pathways were relaid using asphalt, to cater for heavy usage.

New semi-mature trees, about 20 in total, have been planted to complement existing trees at the Osborne Grove and Beatrice Road ends of the Park and to provide screening for the play ground and the hard surfaced play area.

Over 2,000 shrubs and bushes of a variety of species have been planted. Most planting has taken place in the vicinity of the play area and the playground (primarily for screening purposes) and at the Beatrice Road end of the park where there are two avenues of existing mature trees. New seating has been provided along the avenue using treated timber slats, and two lockable litter bins have been provided. The iron railings that once surrounded the park have been removed to make the park more open to the surrounding housing and to 'soften' the formal nature of the park (figures 6 and 7).

The design and planning of the park refurbishment was undertaken by the Parks and Recreation division of the Environment Services Department. Implementation was also undertaken by the Parks and Recreation division with assistance from the Bolton Task Force (MSC – Community Programme labour). Work on Hatfield Road began late in 1983 and was completed in 1984. Responsibility for maintenance rests with the Parks and Recreation Division. Although the refurbishment has substantially improved the appearance and the potential usage of the park there are some

improvements that have not worked so well, for reasons of poor design, materials and implementation. These include the wall to the play area, which already has started to breakaway, and the positioning of new trees in a grassed area (inviting damage from lawnmowers) and close to a football area (inviting damage from children).

Project schedule – Hatfield Road

Early 1980's	Environmental Services Department (Parks and Recreation division) set out policy to refurbish existing parks and create new public open space. Hatfield Road Park selected for improvement.
1982–83	Refurbishment of Hatfield Road Park approved work started.
1984	Work completed.

Costs

The total capital cost of the refurbishment was £19,000. The project was funded through the Urban Programme, 1982/83. Estimated annual revenue expenditure for maintenance work is £4,500.

Beneficiaries

There are approximately 60 households either facing or backing onto Hatfield Road Park, and those residents constitute the main beneficiaries of the park, although there is usage by residents living within an approximate 0.5 to 1 kilometre radius of the park.

General impressions of the improvements to the park were favourable. The new play area and improved play ground were particularly welcomed by parents although there was some criticism of the

47

removal of the railings because of the potential danger to children. There was almost unanimous support for the visual improvements to the park which were particularly welcomed by older residents who enjoy views from their front windows and can take advantage of the new seating. Although only a few residents stated that they now used the park more themselves the Parks and Recreation division believe that there has been a marked increase in usage, especially amongst children, since the park was refurbished.

Overall, the park, despite being small in size, has managed to cater for the needs of both active and passive users and for the wide ranging age groups who live close by.

5 Cannon Street Park, Bolton

Design features

- Grassing and landscaping of housing clearance area
- Blocks of dense planting
- Provision of footpaths
- Level area for ball games
- Childrens play area

Beneficiaries

- Local residents
- Local football clubs

Good practice

- Part of a programme of work to increase the provision of open space by improving derelict land
- Combines facilities for active and passive users
- Successful planting regime
- Low maintenance requirements
- Extensive site allows scope for further improvements.

Key facts

The creation of a new park including a play area and a grassed area for ball games on a housing clearance site in Bolton.

Size:	24,000 square metres
Cost: Capital:	£35,000 1980–81 and £85,000 1983/84
Revenue:	£3,520 per annum maintenance.
Funding sources:	Urban Programme (capital) Bolton MBC (revenue)
Initiator:	Environmental Services Department, Bolton Metropolitan Borough Council.
Implementation:	Environmental Services Department, Bolton Metropolitan Borough Council.

Cannon Street Park is a sizeable new area of public open space less than one kilometre from the centre of Bolton. It forms part of a programme of work undertaken by the Environmental Services Department of Bolton Metropolitan Borough Council designed to increase the amount of public open space in Bolton and to improve existing parks and play areas (*see* HATFIELD ROAD, BOLTON).

The development of a new and sizeable park in an inner urban area is not commonplace and for this reason alone Cannon Street Park has been selected as an example of good practice. The park is also of interest because of its design, which caters for passive and active recreation users, and because it is directly aimed at the open space and recreation needs of a large number of local residents most of whom are public sector tenants.

Origins

Cannon Street Park arose from a strongly held view in the Parks and Recreation division of the Environmental Services Department that the town's inner area was deficient in the provision of public open space and recreation facilities. New areas of open space became a priority objective, especially where there were opportunities to improve neglected and derelict land, and where sites existed close to areas of housing. The derelict housing clearance site in the vicinity of

Cannon Street offered the ideal opportunity to create a sizeable new park that would cater for both active and passive users. The clearance site was adjacent to relatively modern local authority housing and in an areas with little open space or recreation facilities.

Cannon Street Park is, to date, the only totally new park that has been developed under the Park and Recreation division's programme of work.

Design, implementation and maintenance

The site for the park slopes down from the Birkdale housing estate on the southern boundary of the park. The slope, whilst creating some design constraints, has aided drainage and has helped break any monotony in the visual impact of what is a predominantly grassed open space. The slope has meant that the football pitch had to be sited towards the lower end of the park where the slope flattens out, and a children's play area has been constructed on flat ground at the higher end. This location is particularly suitable for a play area being adjacent to the housing estate.

In addition to play facilities almost 200 standard and semi-mature trees of different varieties have been planted around the perimeter of the park and next to the newly created pathways. Over 300 whips and bushes have also been planted on the site with concentrations of planting on the park perimeter.

A key feature of the planting is the presence of

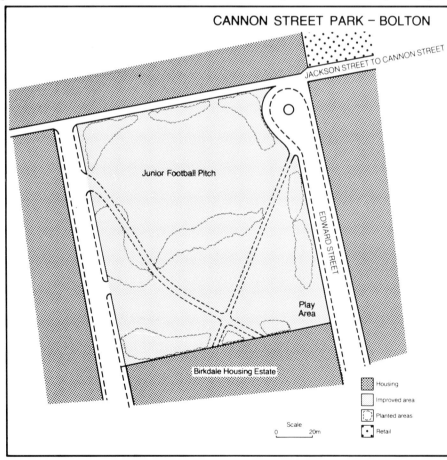

Plan 5: The new park and football pitch at Cannon Street, Bolton

densely planted blocks of whips and bushes. This has the effect of providing a massed and varied area of greenery and allows for some natural losses without substantially detracting from the appearance of the planted areas.

Planting on the perimeter is designed to form a more natural and informal boundary to the park than could be achieved by fencing. The perimeter has been revised by mounding with gaps where appropriate for access. The sense of informality is emphasised further by the lack of park gates or signs advertising the presence of a park. Where fencing exists it divides the rear gardens of the houses of the Birkdale estate from the park. In spite of the open access vandalism is low and there has been little need to replace trees or shrubs.

On the eastern side of the park Jackson Street has been pedestrianised (as a separate project). Jackson Street is the throughroute from Cannon Street Park to the Bolton centre and is heavily used by pedestrians. A footpath links the Birkdale Housing estate to the entrance of Jackson Street, as it was intended from the outset that many of the parks users would be local residents using the park as a route to local and town centre shops (figure 8).

The implementation of the project was undertaken by the Parks and Recreation division of the Environmental Services Department. The division has been involved in all aspects of the work from design through site clearance and laying out the park to maintenance and management. Maintenance mainly consists of grass cutting and care of the football pitch. The main users of the football pitch are local junior clubs.

The project was undertaken in two phases. The first in 1981/82 was concerned with site preparation works, for example, the provision of mounding, following site clearance. The second phase, which included all the planting and landscaping works and the provision of recreation facilities, was completed in 1983.

Figure 8: Tree planting at Cannon Street, and the paths linking housing to local shops

Project schedule – Cannon Street Park

Late 1970's	Policy set out by Bolton MBC to increase the provision of open space and recreational facilities in the inner area.
1981	Design of Cannon Street Park on a housing clearance area.
1981/82	Basic site works undertaken (Phase One).
1983	Completion of landscaping works and provision of recreational facilities (Phase Two).

Costs

The costs for the two phases were

Phase One	1980/81	£35,900	Site preparation works
Phase Two	1983/84	£85,000	Landscaping, footpaths, play areas and football pitch.

Beneficiaries

The residents of a relatively newly built public housing estate adjoining the open space welcomed this project. They all remembered the vacant area left after the housing had been cleared and saw the grassing and planting as a substantial improvement. Most of the residents used the new area of open space both as an amenity in its own right and as a through route to Cannon Street and into central Bolton. The provision and the quality of footpaths were especially welcomed by parents with prams or pushchairs, who also valued the playground because of its nearness to their homes. Not surprisingly, those living the furthest from the play area would have liked it to have been more centrally situated within the mark.

Residents commented on additional improvements that could be undertaken on this site, including individual gateways from homes backing onto the park, a second football pitch and a row of benches on the higher level to enable residents to enjoy views across the centre of Bolton towards the Pennines.

The size of the park and the large grassland area not currently used for ball games allow scope for further development of Cannon Street Park. The Parks and Recreation division already have plans for future improvements including additional planting and fencing work using MSC labour. At the same time discussions with the Bolton Education Department may result in school playing fields on part of the site.

6   Green's Gardens, Nottingham

Design features

- Use of materials to harmonise with restored mill.

- Dense planting for visual impact.

- Industrial machinery for historic effect.

Beneficiaries

- Local residents and their children.

- Education institutions using the mill museum as a resource.

- The people of Nottingham

Good practice

- Effective use of windmill as a centrepiece.

- Good co-ordination between local authority departments and the local community.

- Provision of an educational resource.

- Effective re-use of old mill machinery as part of the landscaping.

- Combines facilities for active and passive users.

- Strong visual impact.

- Community involvement.

- Diversity of funding.

- Meets environmental, recreational, education and conservation objectives.

Key facts

A restored windmill provides the centre piece for a landscaped local amenity area which includes a play area for small children.

Size:	8,000 square metres
Cost: Capital:	£132,000 (1981-6)
Revenue:	Estimated at £2,000 per annum for maintenance.
Funding sources:	Urban Programme (£50,000) City of Nottingham (£45,000 + revenue) Civic Society (£6,000) George Green Memorial Fund (£20,000) City of Nottingham Lottery (£10,000) Civic Trust (£500)
Initiator:	George Green Memorial Fund and Planning Department, Nottingham City Council.
Implementation:	Departments of Planning, Recreation, Technical Services and Arts, Nottingham City Council using MSC labour and private contractors.

The land, which has come to be known as Green's Gardens, covers an area of 0.8 hectares and has been used as allotments since the beginning of the 20th Century. An early 19th century red brick tower windmill, which can be seen from vantage points around Nottingham, forms a focal point on the brow of a hill in the northern part of the site. The windmill fell into disuse in the latter part of the 19th century and gradually into disrepair, losing all its machinery floors in a fire in 1949. The restored windmill is now the centrepiece of a landscaped local amenity area that has aroused interest and enthusiasm throughout Nottingham.

Origins

Nottingham City Council undertook a wide ranging study of the rundown residential area of Sneinton, which is situated within the inner urban area, about a kilometre from the city centre. A local plan was prepared for the improvement of Sneinton and one of its proposals was the complete restoration of the Green's Gardens windmill to working order and the landscaping of surrounding land to provide much needed open space and play facilities for young children.

The windmill has historic significance. George Green, a renowned physicist, who contributed to the development of electrical and electronic engineering, lived in the windmill for the greater part of his life. The idea of restoring the windmill as a memorial to this eminent scientist was mooted at an International Conference on Physics in Budapest in 1974, attended by some 800 delegates. The George Green Memorial Fund was subsequently established, and sufficient funds had been raised by 1978 for the mill and its immediate curtilage to be purchased with the aid of a grant from the Civic Trust. The Fund then donated the windmill and its surroundings to the City Council, who had agreed to co-ordinate the restoration of the windmill with the purchase and landscaping of Green's Gardens as a public park with a well equipped play area. Proposals for the museum within the confines of the mill buildings were prepared by the Department of Technical Services, Nottingham City Council and officers from this department have also taken the lead in implementing a car park which serves both Green's Gardens and an adjoining community hall. Whilst essentially part of the Green's Gardens project the community hall was the subject of a separate (voluntary sector) bid for Urban Programme funding. The restoration of the semi-derelict hall for use as a vistor centre was carried out by Community Task Force labour working to the Planning Department.

When originally conceived the plans were to pro-

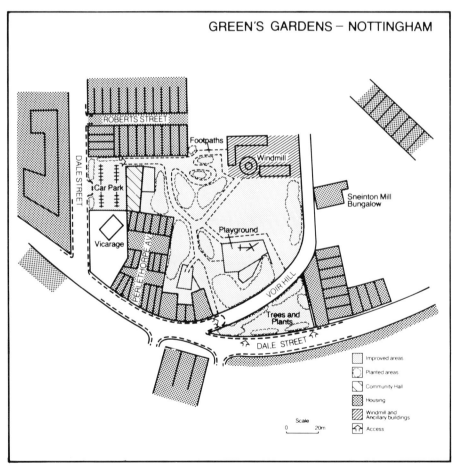

Plan 6: Green's Gardens, Nottingham.

vide a 'standard' landscaping treatment for the amenity areas of the site with a budget allocation from the City's Recreation Department. However, popular interest in the mill's restoration, coupled with the opportunities presented by the advent of the Urban Programme, provided the impetus and the finance for a more elaborate scheme. A higher quality landscaping project was subsequently implemented by the Recreation Department.

Design and implementation

The outline drawings show the location of the two main features within Green's Gardens: the windmill and the play area. Other notable features include the refurbished community hall and car parking provision which also serves the windmill. Old milling machinery has been used to help landscape the site and to provide a reminder of Green's Gardens associations with industrial history. Further reminders are provided by a grinding stone and an information plate on the main pedestrian access to the site.

The materials used throughout the scheme harmonise with the restored windmill. Reclaimed timbers, bricks and setts have been used to good effect for hard landscaping features (figure 9). Most notable amongst these are the timber edging to the shrub planted areas, the setts supporting the slide and the multi-function timber climbing frame in the older children's play area.

The land sloping down from the windmill has been grassed. There is dense planting of trees and bushes on the periphery of the site, and also alongside the footpaths that have been laid to provide access to the site and to link the mill to the landscaped and play areas. Seating has been provided at various locations in the landscaped area.

The Department of Recreation implemented the play area and landscaping works using private con-

Figure 9: Reclaimed timbers, bricks and setts have been used to good effect for hard landscaping and play equipment

tractors. Restoration of the mill was started under the direction of the Departments of Planning and Recreation, guided by a mill wright leading a team of MSC trainees. The Technical Services and Arts Departments became involved when the decision was made to provide a museum in new buildings forming a courtyard around the restored mill.

Project schedule – Green's Gardens

1974	George Green Memorial Fund established.
1978	Green's Gardens site acquired by Nottingham City Council; low budget landscaping scheme drawn up.
1979/80	Project included in approved submission; restoration of mill began.
May 1980	Purchase of 0.13 ha of land from County Council to complete project space.
1980	Detailed project plans drawn up.
August 1981– Sept 1983	Play area and landscaping works implemented; mill restoration continued.
1983–5	Car park implemented; community hall refurbished.
1986	Windmill completed; museum fully operational.

Cost

The estimated cost of restoration was £132,000 of which only £50,000 was intended to be derived from the Urban Programme. Other sources of finance have been used; £10,000 was raised under the City Lottery and £20,000 came through the George Green Memorial Appeal, supported by a wide range of individuals and institutions. A further £6,000 was raised by the local Civic Society which nominated the project for a Civic Trust 'Pride of Place' award from which it received an additional £500. Allocations have been made from the main programme budgets of the Planning Department and the Arts Department, which will administer the museum on the ground floor of the restored windmill.

Maintenance costs have been estimated to be in the order of £2,000 per annum. The planting regime has had relatively few natural losses.

Beneficiaries

Restoration of Green's windmill has caught the imagination of many people in Nottingham and had it

Figure 10: The Windmill creates a focus, and old machinery links the park to its industrial history.

not been retained a piece of industrial heritage might otherwise have been lost to them (figure 10). The conversion of the groundfloor of the windmill to a museum provides a local point of interest and educational resource for educational institutions both within Nottingham and further away.

A majority of residents interviewed spoke favourably of the Green's Gardens scheme. Indeed, 90% said that it had made Sneinton a better place in which to live. Residents with children benefit from the play area since there was no adequate facilities for safe play before. Elderly residents in particular enjoy the landscaping on the site and the views of Nottingham afforded by the provision of seating.

People have started to visit the windmill from all over Nottingham. The prospect of good custom has encouraged the publican of an adjoining public house to provide a beer garden with access to Green's Gardens.

A range of benefits have been derived from the retention of a building of historic significance as an integrated part of a scheme which has combined educational, amenity and social objectives. Cooperation between local authority departments has been a key figure in attaining benefits and meeting objectives.

7 Potternewton Park, Leeds

<table>
<tr><td>

Design features

- Renovation of three existing tennis courts.

- Conversion of two existing tennis courts to basketball courts.

- New walled kickabout area.

- Additional drainage.

Beneficiaries

- Local residents.

- Schools in the vicinity.

Good practice

- Public consultation.

- Responded to ethnic minority needs.

- Responded to priority area objectives.

- Imaginative re-use of materials in the new play area.

- Low maintenance requirements.

- Innovative use of soft surrounds for play equipment.

</td><td>

Key facts

General improvements and refurbishment of a traditionally laid out Victorian park. Play areas have been upgraded and additional facilities provided.

Size: 110,000 square metres

Cost: Capital: £31,330 (1982-4)

Revenue: Estimated annual maintenance cost of £3,330.

Funding sources: Urban Programme (Capital) Leeds City Council (Revenue)

Initiator: Leisure Services Department, Leeds City Council.

Implementation: Leisure Services Department, Leeds City Council.

</td></tr>
</table>

Many towns and cities have 'traditional' town parks which were laid out in the Victorian era. Potternewton Park, which is situated within the Chapeltown district of Leeds, is one such park. With its expansive grassy slopes, traversed by tree lined walkways, Potternewton Park has formed the 'green lungs' of this part of Leeds for many years.

However, the park was becoming increasingly rundown, drainage in the lower reaches of the park was a problem and one of the walkways was lined with the unsafe remains of wartime air raid shelters. The existing facilities were well used but in need of attention.

Improvements were undertaken in response to perceived needs and expressed demands of the local community. With its existing facilities upgraded and additional facilities provided the park now enjoys a new lease of life (figure 11). A new vitality has been brought to a well established amenity through a relatively low cost scheme.

Origins

Potternewton Park is situated within the Chapeltown district of inner Leeds. The City Council established Chapeltown as a priority for the concentration of Urban Programme resources in 1980. The area's unique character and problems are reflected in poor housing conditions and high unemployment which together contributed to a worsening environment and rundown appearance.

Chapeltown largely dates from the nineteenth century and consists of large family houses, which have become multi-occupied and, in many cases, poorly maintained. The local community consists of over forty different ethnic groups including the largest number of residents of West Indian origin in the city. Unemployment is high and the lack of achievement and motivation amongst teenagers continues to pose a serious problem.

It is against this background and in the context of policies to ameliorate these problems that proposals were put forward for a number of environmental schemes in the area. The Leisure Services Department of the City Council selected the Potternewton Park scheme because it offered an opportunity to upgrade well used facilities and scope for meeting local needs and those of local ethnic groups in particular.

Public consultation was undertaken to canvass opinions on the proposals to upgrade the existing play facilities and tennis courts. Problems of drainage and the requirement to provide other facilities, which more closely matched local needs, were brought to the attention of the City Council. A modified scheme subsequently received City Council approval and was included within the 1981 Urban Programme submission for implementation in 1982/3.

Design and implementation

Potternewton Park, which is approximately 11 hectares in size, had three popular bowling greens situated towards the eastern side of the park. These were and remain neatly laid out, with well maintained privet hedges and rose beds.

A large area of tarmacadam, divided into five tennis courts, adjoined the bowling greens (figure 12). During the refurbishment works this was resurfaced, new netting was erected and two of the tennis courts were converted for use as basketball courts. The response to demands from local groups for more varied sporting facilities within the park also encouraged the provision of a walled kickabout area.

The existing swings were replaced and additional play equipment was provided. This included a brightly coloured bus-shaped climber, a slide, a see-saw and a roundabout. Effective use was made of recycled materials, including sandstone setts, telegraph poles and railway sleepers as hard landscaping features of the play area design (figure 13). Signifi-

Figure 11: The mixture of old trees and slopes with new facilities

Figure 12: The park provides for a variety of recreational needs

Figure 13: The play area uses recycled materials and has soft surfaces surrounding the play equipment. It cannot stop rain!

cantly, all the play area design equipment is encircled by soft surface material to avoid unnecessary injury. The play area is separated from the kickabout area to provide separate play areas for younger children and teenagers.

In addition to the sport and play facilities drainage problems in the lower parts of the site were resolved. An area in the vicinity of the air raid shelters was made safe, hollows were filled, regraded and grassed. Originally it had been intended to remove the air raid shelters but the cost would have borne little relation to the benefits derived.

Project schedule – Potternewton Park

May 1981	Chapeltown established as a Priority Area.
October 1981	Scheme included in IAP Submission for implementation 1982/3.
December 1982	Improvements began.
October 1983	Completion of programmed works.

Costs

All the refurbishment works were undertaken by the City Council's leisure services department between December 1982 and October 1983. The final cost of £31,330 slightly exceeded the original estimate of £30,000.

The capital costs can be itemised as follows:

(i)	Tennis court renovation and conversion of others to provide basket ball courts	£12,148
(ii)	Conversion of former tennis court area to a walled kickabout area	£11,758
(iii)	Miscellaneous works (including drainage, resurfacing of footpaths, soiling and seeding and sealing off the former air raid shelter)	£3,037
(iv)	Trim trail	£1,150
(v)	Administration and Fees	£3,237

The maintenance of Potternewton Park is undertaken by the Leisure Services department as part of their programme of maintenance for parks in Leeds. The estimated annual maintenance cost associated with the park refurbishment is £3,328.

Beneficiaries

The refurbishment works have upgraded existing sports and play provision and enhanced the image of a park in a rundown area. In addition, the provision of extra sporting and play facilities has benefited local residents. Indeed, all those interviewed felt that the improvements had made Chapeltown a better area in which to live.

Local schools take advantage of the tennis, basketball and kickabout spaces and the play area is particularly popular amongst mothers with children. One mother spoken to had travelled to Potternewton Park by car in order that her child might use the play area. Another mother regularly brought her child to the park as it was 'the best play area around'.

Housing related improvements

8   Black Patch, Sandwell

Design features

- Housing related soft and hard landscaping.

- Provision of gardens for ground floor flats.

- Provision of a landscaped safety area.

- New drying and car parking areas.

- Low maintenance planting regime.

Beneficiaries

- Local residents.

Good practice

- Public consultation.

- Linked to district wide policy of housing related environmental improvements.

- Co-ordination between local authority departments and the residents aided by presence of community landscape architect.

- Successful planting regime.

- Community involvement.

- Mix of Urban Programme and Main Programme Funding.

Key facts

Landscaping and other environmental improvements undertaken within a small public sector housing estate in Sandwell. A community landscape architect was employed to take account of the ideas and preferences of residents.

Size: Small housing estate, approximately 200 dwellings.

Cost: Capital: £102,400 1984–86 on environmental improvements. An additional £53,800 has been spent on the refurbishment of Black Patch Park and £154,500 on the building of a community centre.

Revenue: £16,500 p.a. to cover costs of community landscape architect and maintenance.

Funding sources: Urban Programme capital funding and £12,000 p.a. revenue funding for community landscape architect (continuing post with a varying proportion of time spent on Black Patch estate).
Sandwell MBC, Housing Department £10,000 (environmental improvements).
Sandwell, MBC Recreation and Amenities Department, revenue.

Initiator: Recreation and Amenities Department and Housing Department, Sandwell Metropolitan Borough Council.

Implementation: Recreation and Amenities Department and Housing Department, Sandwell Metropolitan Borough Council.

Black Patch is a small (just over 200 households) and isolated area of public sector housing on the boundary of Sandwell and the City of Birmingham. To the north and east are the Handsworth and Winson Green areas of Birmingham. Railway lines enclose the estate on three sides with industry forming a barrier on the fourth. Black Patch, due to its general and specific location, had become an enclave that was neither properly part of Sandwell or Birmingham. The housing stock, a mixture of pre and post war four storey tenament blocks, had been deteriorating for some years. Unemployment levels in the area were amongst the highest in Sandwell. There were also areas of dereliction close to the estate and the provision of facilities and environmental amenities was particularly lacking. Overall, the image of Black Patch was poor and the estate was unpopular with existing and potential tenants (figure 14).

The approach adopted by Sandwell MBC to alleviate the environmental problems of Black Patch is innovative and interesting. This is largely because the improvements at Black Patch have been undertaken as a co-ordinated programme of work which has involved the Recreation and Amenities, the Housing and the Education departments as well as local residents. Sandwell MBC appointed a community landscape architect to work almost exclusively on the improvements to Black Patch and to involve local residents wherever possible.

Figure 14: Black Patch estate as it was before improvement

Origins

Sandwell MBC recognised the problems of Black Patch and the need to halt and reverse the decline of the estate. At the same time it was also recognised that the relatively small and distinct area of Black Patch gave an ideal opportunity for a series of co-ordinated improvements that would seek to address the problems of the housing stock, the lack of facilities and the run down environment. It was agreed that Sandwell Housing Department would give Black Patch priority for bring-

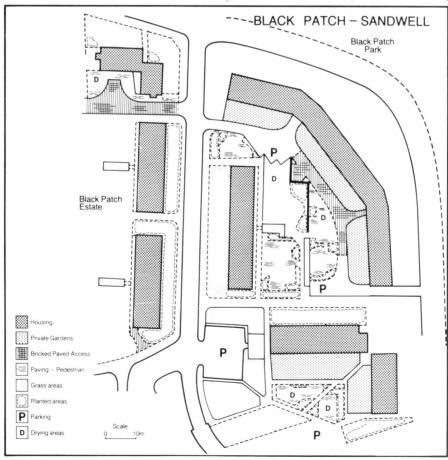

Plan 7: Landscaping and environmental improvements at Black Patch estate

ing outstanding repairs and improvements up to date. At the same time the Recreation and Amenities Department would manage a range of improvements that included the refurbishment of Black Patch Park, the provision of parking spaces, and hard and soft landscaping works. The Department of Technical Services played an initial role by overseeing the reclamation of Merryhill, a derelict area on the southern boundary of the estate. As a result of this reclamation there is now a visual barrier between most of the housing on the estate and the Birmingham to Wolverhampton railway line.

For any improvements to Black Patch to be successful it was considered essential to win over local support in the light of high levels of vandalism and a low level of confidence in the area.

The situation demanded a link between the community and the local authority so that priorities and needs could be determined and support could be canvassed. The scale of the problem justified assigning an officer to work virtually full time to design and set in motion improvements for Black Patch Estate. As Sandwell did not have resources or staff available a successful bid was made through the Urban Programme for the funding of a community landscape architect. The resultant post is continuing and is based within the Recreation and Amenities Department.

Design, implementation and maintenance

The community landscape architect undertook vital consultations both with the Black Patch Tenants' Association (who were highly sceptical at the outset) and with individual residents. As a result of these discussions the following priorities were developed for the programme of improvements:

(i) the need for limited car parking areas, and safer routes for pedestrians;

(ii) the preference for specific landscaping improvements between housing blocks, and directly adjacent to housing not on the periphery of the estate; and

(iii) a desire for 'defensible space' in the form of separate drying areas for each housing block and where possible for individual gardens.

Inevitably, the residents' concern centred on the condition of the housing stock. The presence of the community landscape architect allowed residents to express some of their concerns directly to a local government officer. As a result, housing improvements, and repairs in particular, have largely kept pace with environmental improvements.

In addition to meeting the needs and preferences of residents, the local authority wanted to ensure that the improvements undertaken, were both durable and relatively free from maintenance. In practice this coincided with the preferences of the residents for

Figure 15: Improvements have included fenced gardens and courtyards, brick paving, planting and drying areas

'defensible space' and for improvements directly adjacent to housing blocks which, it was felt, would increase local pride on the estate and reduce vandalism.

The outcome has been a policy of planting trees and shrubs on what were the grassed areas between housing blocks, so as to reduce maintenance costs and provide a visual change in the local environment. A separate car parking area has been created to avoid the dangers to children playing. This danger has been further reduced by the provision of a small play area to the rear of one of the housing blocks. Twelve separate drying areas with rotary dryers have been provided. Pathways between housing blocks have been repaired to a high quality finish, using brick in some cases (figure 15).

For those living on the ground floor, rear gardens have been extended wherever possible and areas in front of some flats have been fenced off to create small gardens or courtyards.

The work was undertaken in two phases. Initially work centred on a small distinct area of the estate. When this had been successfully implemented it was used as a model for the remainder of the estate.

Project schedule – Black Patch

1983	Idea initiated by Recreation and Amenities, and Housing Departments, Sandwell MBC.
1984	Phase 1. Environmental Improvements undertaken on part of the estate.
1985–86	Appointment of Community Landscape Architect. Phase 2. Improvements extended to cover all of the estate. Refurbishment of Black Patch Park; construction of community centre.
1986	Extension of Black Patch experiment to other estates in Sandwell.

In addition to the environmental improvements on the estate, and the improvements to the housing stock, the Recreation and Amenities Department has secured Urban Programme finance to refurbish Black Patch Park. The park is located to the immediate north of the estate and covers an area of 7 hectares. The improvements to Black Patch Park were started once the improvements to the estate were well advanced. Work on the park is now complete and involves a BMX track, a cricket table, a new play area, improved paths and a car park with a 15 car capacity.

To improve the community facilities on the estate the Recreation and Amenities, and the Education Departments of Sandwell MBC have jointly funded the development of a new community centre. The centre is located within Black Patch Park.

The responsibility for implementing the improvements both to the estate and the park rests with the Recreation and Amenities Department. However, the work involving construction activities, hard landscaping and fencing was contracted out, predominantly to local specialist firms. The work was undertaken in two phases between 1984 and 1986. Once the first phase had been successfully implemented similar improvements were undertaken throughout the estate.

Maintenance of the environmental improvements is undertaken by the Recreation and Amenities Department and is largely confined to grass cutting which is undertaken in conjunction with maintenance work at Black Patch Park. The planted areas have become established with few losses and are relatively maintenance free. However, recently there have been signs of vandalism reoccurring with the rotary driers being particular objects of the vandals' attention.

Costs

The Urban Programme has been the main source of funding for the improvements to Black Patch. The hard and soft landscaping works (including rotary driers, car parking areas on the estate, and fencing) cost £102,400 between 1984 and 1986. Of this, £10,000 was derived for the Housing Department's main programme (the Housing Department have also funded repairs and improvements to the housing stock). The remainder of the capital works were funded through the Urban Programme.

The Community Landscape Architect (a continuing post) has been financed by Urban Programme revenue support at £12,000 per annum. About 85% of his time was, until the end of 1985, spent on the Black Patch improvement programme. The estimated annual cost of environmental maintenance is £4,000 which includes maintenance in Black Patch Park. Maintenance work is funded by the Recreation and Amenities Department.

Beneficiaries

When local residents were first consulted about proposed improvements there was a high level of scepticism. Following the years of neglect the Tenants' Association were not convinced of the local authority's intentions. The speed with which Sandwell acted and the appointment of a community landscape architect to work as a link between the residents and the local authority managed to allay most of the doubts. The views of local residents, at the end of the first phase of the improvements, were generally positive and favourable.

Residents were particularly appreciative of the provision of rotary dryers, the fencing of common and private space, and the provision of car parking which helped to keep cars away from the parts of the estate most used by children. Most residents interviewed had been involved with the work of the community landscape architect and some had been directly involved in the improvement works. There appeared to be a high level of local pride in what had been achieved with residents keeping watch over the drying areas and the planting between housing blocks. The general impression was of a neater, tidier area. A small number of residents cited the improvements as a main reason for staying on the estate.

More recently there have been some signs of deterioration. The number of vacant properties were reduced initially but are now rising, in common with the rest of the borough, and vandalism which was low during the implementation of the project is now more evident. There is also a general view amongst residents interviewed that whilst the efforts of the Parks and Recreation department are appreciated more fundamental issues such as the condition of housing, unemployment and the lack of shops and services still adversely affect the quality of life in Black Patch.

The project illustrates that whilst improvements to the environment alone cannot solve social and economic problems they can make an important contribution improving the quality of life. In particular Sandwell MBC point to the improved relationships with the stimulation of interest amongst local residents. The minor deficiencies of the Black Patch project have arisen from design and implementation details, for example the unprotected location of rotary driers, and not from the philosophy underpinning the approach. The community landscape architect has been retained to repeat the Black Patch experiment on other estates in Sandwell but is still available to, and still contacted by, residents of Black Patch wishing to suggest further improvements or to report the need for repairs. This, in itself, is evidence of the achievement of the Black Patch project in improving the interest and awareness of residents in their local environment.

9 Hylton Dene, Sunderland

Design features

- Substantial tree planting.
- Pathway provision.
- Debris clearance.
- Stream outfall mechanism replaced.
- Concrete bridge.

Beneficiaries

- Residents in the vicinity.
- Schoolchildren and pedestrians
- The people of Sunderland.

Good practice

- Public consultation.
- Good use of existing woodland area.
- Involvement of school children and students.
- Innovative approach to maintenance.
- Low maintenance requirements.
- Significant potential for future development.

Key facts

A scheme to improve access to, and the appearance and usefulness of, an extensive area of poor quality open space and woodland in the heart of a densely populated area.

Size:		300,000 square metres.
Cost:	*Capital:*	£117,000 1981–85.
	Revenue:	Estimated cost of maintenance required per annum £10,000. Actual expenditure on maintenance 1985/6 £7,578.
Funding sources:		Urban Programme (capital) Borough of Sunderland (revenue).
Initiator:		Planning Department, Borough of Sunderland.
Implementation:		Department of Works, Borough of Sunderland.

A paucity of mature tree cover is a characteristic of many urban areas and may be regarded as a major landscape deficiency. Hylton Dene, in the Castletown district of Sunderland, was formerly dense woodland but neglect has led to significant losses in recent years. A concerted programme of new planting, replacement and woodland management has now been undertaken and the recreational value of an extensive (30 ha.) corridor of green space is now being realised.

Origins

Sunderland has a number of large peripheral housing estates, which whilst not visually dominated by high rise dwellings, exhibit relatively high unemployment levels, associated social problems and have a distinct lack of amenity open space.

In the local plan for this northern part of the Borough, Sunderland's Planning Department specified that Hylton Dene was underused and an unrealised asset. This was due, in part, to restricted access to the area which had long been associated with a working colliery system. Indeed, the lower reaches of the Dene were still owned by the National Coal Board, which wished to retain an option to build a coal liquidification plant. More recently much of the area had become an eyesore with substantial and indiscriminate flytipping (figure 16).

Figure 16: Hylton Dene prior to improvement, an area few people wanted to use.

Councillors from the Castletown ward were keen to see progress made on improvements to Hylton Dene, because the higher reaches of the site extended into the housing estates and improvements would bring obvious community benefits.

A consultation exercise was organised by the Borough Planning Department to gauge the opinions of residents and local schools. This brought forward

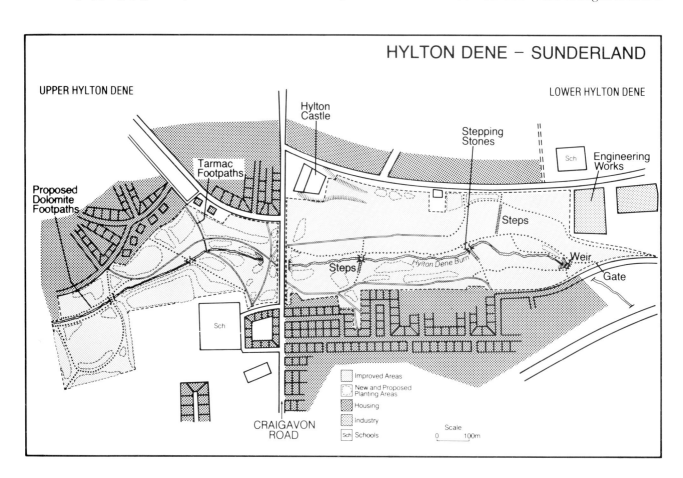

Plan 8: Hylton Dene, Sunderland

positive suggestions, particularly on the direction of footpaths and the position of a footbridge to cross the stream which runs the length of Hylton Dene.

Information on local flora and fauna was sought from the Nature Conservancy Council, who advised that a hay meadow, situated away from housing, lower down the Dene, was of special interest. Other notable features of this more isolated area of the Dene were thorn breaks and rare water lillies.

Design, implementation and maintenance

Following these consultations a master plan was prepared for the whole Hylton Dene corridor. It was anticipated that initial emphasis would be placed on the areas nearest the housing, although improvements could take place throughout the site. The Planning Department's stated objective was to 'generally improve the access to, appearance and usefulness of an extensive area of open space and woodland', which did not necessitate a complex scheme. Rather simple functional improvements characterise the landscape design for Hylton Dene.

First, large quanities of rubble and rubbish that had been dumped were cleared. Successive years of tipping had reduced soil quality. To improve conditions for growth the ground was extensively rotorvated.

Footpaths and pedestrian footbridges were laid out in the directions local residents had suggested. The footpaths, of tarmac and dolomite, were constructed to both improve access to the Dene and conditions underfoot. Crossing Hylton Dene burn was made easier by the construction of wooden footbridges and steps. Fire subsequently destroyed the footbridge in the upper area of the Dene. The footbridge is now constructed of concrete with metal railings for durability. In an effort to further improve conditions underfoot considerable resources were directed towards improving drainage. This involved the replacement of storm water discharges and outfall mechanisms associated with the flood control of Hylton Dene burn.

Extensive tree planting has taken place throughout Hylton Dene (figure 17). Indigenous species such as beech have been used to provide ground cover in the upper areas. Closely planted whips have been used and it has been necessary to fence these to deter vandalism. Elsewhere in the Dene replacement tree planting has taken place and woodland management measures have been undertaken.

The first phase of work commenced in late 1981 and was completed in 1985. A second phase, which involves creative woodland management, building upon the first phase improvements is the subject of separate Urban Programme funding. The Department of Works was responsible for implementing the first phase and community involvement is being encouraged during the second.

Maintenance has been undertaken by the Depart-

Figure 17: Woodland in the lower Dene was better established but has been supplemented by new trees, bushes and general landscaping.

ment of Works but Sunderland Polytechnic students and local schools have been encouraged to become involved in the management of the woodland areas of Hylton Dene.

Project schedule – Hylton Dene

1979	North Area District Plan published; noted Hylton Dene underdeveloped and underused.
1980	Project within approved IAP submission though strictly outside the Inner Area.
October 1981	Clearance of rubble and rubbish.
1982/3	Repair of stream outfall mechanism.
1983/5	First phase of project implemented.

Costs

The capital costs associated with the scheme total £117,000. These costs are broken down as follows:

(i) Site clearance works including removal of quantities of rubble and rubbish: £15,000, 1981/2.

(ii) Improvements to the storm damage systems and water courses: £37,000, 1982/3.

(iii) Provision of footpaths, steps and bridges: £35,000, 1983/4.

(iv) Ground preparations and planting: £30,000, 1984/5.

All capital costs were funded through the Urban Programme.

The revenue requirements associated with maintenance are estimated by the Borough of Sunderland to be £10,000 per annum. Actual expenditure on maintenance in 1985/86 was £7,578.

Beneficiaries

The residents of Castletown are the main beneficiaries of this improvement project. Deficiency in open space provision in the area has meant that the improvements in access and appearance of the area adjacent to housing has been particularly well received. Indeed, the majority of residents questioned felt that the works undertaken provided a significant visual improvement. Over half the residents spoken to felt that the improvement had made the area a better place in which to live. Many recognised that further benefits would be derived when the trees and planting mature and become better established.

Local schools have been encouraged to become involved in the development of Hylton Dene. Elements of the site have educational potential and this has been outlined as part of a package, including information boards, that has been presented by the Planning Department. Sunderland Polytechnic students and local schools have become involved in the management of the woodland areas of Hylton Dene, undertaking planting and other activities as part of courses in environmental studies.

Hylton Dene offers significant potential for the future, particularly if wider community involvement in the second phase of management can be encouraged. Retention of the hay meadow and other features of natural interest together with close proximity to Hylton Castle offer significant potential for the future.

10 Broughton High and Ascension, Salford

Design features

- All weather multi-use playing area and flood-lit pitch.
- Caretaker's house.
- Football pitches.
- General landscaping of site.
- Semi mature and mature trees to provide immediate impact.

Beneficiaries

- Local residents.
- Local school children.

Good practice

- Good co-ordination between Planning, Education and Recreation Departments.
- High quality planting and surfaces to reduce maintenance costs.
- Combines facilities for active and passive users.
- Planting regime gives visual impact.
- Meets recreational, educational and environmental objectives.
- Site offers potential for further improvement.

Key facts

The reclamation of a housing clearance area in Salford to provide new public open space and play areas for dual usage by local schools and the community.

Size: 50,000 square metres.

Cost: Capital: Phase One £54,000 1978/79.
Phase Two £266,000 1982/83
An additional £197,775 (Derelict Land Grant) 1982/83.

Revenue: No estimates for maintenance costs for the site.

Funding sources: Urban Programme £54,000 (1978/79) and £266,000 (1982/83)
Derelict Land Grant £197,775 (1982/83)
Salford City Council (revenue).

Initiator: Town Clerks and Recreation Departments, Salford City Council.

Implementation: Recreation, Planning and Education Departments' Salford City Council.

Broughton High and Ascension is a predominantly residential area about a kilometre from the centre of Salford. The area is made up of terraced and high rise housing centred around Broughton High School and the Ascension Church of England Primary School. The provision of open space landscaping and recreational facilities was, however, very limited.

The Broughton High and Ascension project sought to rectify this deficiency by providing a substantial area of public open space (5 hectares) primarily for recreational usage but with the addition of landscaping and pathways. Other aspects of good practice in this project include the provision of a caretaker's house, which allows for permanent supervision of the site, and the efforts to forge a closer relationship between the school and the local community via the dual use of sports facilities.

Origins
The Broughton High and Ascension project has developed out of two broad objectives. Firstly, the Manchester – Salford Inner City Partnership has an objective of increasing the provision of public open space in the inner city. In 1977 a total of 293 hectares of public open space existed in the Partnership area. By 1981 this total had increased to 696 hectares largely through Urban Programme funded initiatives. Secondly, Salford City Council, as an education and recreation authority, have a policy of providing new and extending existing playground and recreational facilities, with the intention of promoting dual (school and general public) usage.

Housing adjacent to the two schools had been designated a slum clearance area and this offered Salford an opportunity to extend the recreational facilities of the area and to provide a new area of open space. At the same time it also provided an opportunity to provide soft landscaping in a generally run down environment lacking in greenery.

The Recreation Department of Salford City Council, having responsibility for the provision of outdoor sports, ensured the inclusion of a recreation and public open space project for Broughton High and Ascension in the Lower Broughton Local Plan. Finance was sought and approved from the then new Urban Programme (via the Manchester-Salford Partnership) and initial work began in 1978.

Design, implementation and maintenance
The scale and diversity of the work dictated that the design for the Broughton High and Ascension project should be phased over a period of time.

Phase one, (1978–1979) involved the building of a caretaker's house and the provision of a hard surfaced multi-use play area (figure 18). This play area can be used either for football or it could be subdivided into tennis courts, five-a-side football pitches, or netball

Figure 18: Phase 1 involved building a caretaker's house (left) and a hard multi-use surface (right).

and basketball courts. The surface is of high quality to cater for heavy usage. At the same time a programme of housing clearance was undertaken adjacent to the schools. Work also began on the construction of a Sports Centre next to Broughton High School. The Sport Centre is a separate project jointly initiated by the Education and Recreation Departments of Salford City Council and funded through the Urban Programme. It helps meet the objective of the City Council to improve the provision of recreation facilities in Salford.

The second phase of the work was approved in 1981 and was completed in 1983. This phase comprised the provision of an all weather floodlit pitch, the extension of school playgrounds, an extensive grassed area capable of supporting five football pitches, general landscaping works including peripheral planting and the provision of footpaths.

The provision of the grassed area involved the closure of a roadway (present until housing clearance) and the diversion of underground services (eg drains, gas and water). This aspects of the work proved more problematic, expensive and time consuming than originally estimated.

As the primary objective of the project was recreational the overall design is functional rather than elaborate. Whilst recognising the constraints imposed by the provision of recreational facilities, some immediate and strong visual features were needed to reduce the monotony of an open, flat, grassed area. To this end Salford decided that high quality semi-mature and mature trees and bushes would form the basis of the landscaping programme (figure 19). The footpaths were constructed using asphalt and those on the perimeters of the open space were bordered by shrubs and other plants.

The overall development of the project was the responsibility of the Town Clerk's Department. The design and planning stages of the work were under-

Figure 19: Bushes and semi-mature trees reduce the visual monotony of the flat, open playing fields.

taken jointly by Salford City Council Recreation and Education Departments. Staff at Broughton High School were regularly consulted during the planning stages on both the recreational and landscaping proposals. The implementation of the project was undertaken by an outside contractor, except for the works involving road closures and diversions, which were carried out by the Direct Labour Department of Salford City Council.

Maintenance of the project is undertaken by the Recreation Department (primarily responsible for the grassed areas, football pitches and the landscaping) and the Education Department (responsible for playgrounds and play areas). Although there has been some vandalism on the site, this has reduced considerably as the project has developed. Salford City Council takes the view that the presence of a caretaker on the site, together with the closed circuit television employed by the Sports Centre (part of Salford's anti-vandalism programme) has helped to reduce general vandalism in the area.

Project schedule – Broughton High and Ascension

1978	Plans put forward in the lower Broughton plan for an area of green space and recreational facilities implemented by Salford City Council.
1978–79	Building of caretaker's house and multi-use playing area. Sports centre developed as a separate project. Programme of Housing clearance undertaken between Broughton High and Ascension Primary Schools.
1985	Football pitches useable having been allowed to settle.

Costs
Phase one of the project was undertaken in 1978/79 at a cost of £54,000 (Urban Programme for site clearance after demolition of the housing), the infrastructure works and the provision of subsoil and top soil was funded through Derelict Land Grant at a cost of £197,775 (1982/83). Phase Two of the project was undertaken in 1982 and 1983 and cost £266,000 (Urban Programme). The project has implications on the Recreation and Education Departments' (Salford City Council) maintenance budget although, as the project is absorbed into the programme of maintenance work for the Recreation and Education Departments, it is not possible to accurately estimate the revenue implications associated with the project. Indeed as the grassed football pitches have only recently come into use the full maintenance implications have yet to be realised. However, the quality of the planting and the surfaces of the recreation areas are designed to reduce the costs of maintenance.

Beneficiaries
Both the Ascension Primary and the Broughton High schools were pleased with the work that had been undertaken and the facilities now provided. Both schools also made use of the Sports Centre facilities and looked forward to being able to make regular use of the grassed area for football and cricket. The arrangements for dual usage with the general public (evenings and holidays) are working well, and the playgrounds and play areas are generally well used. The provision of the Sports Centre complements the open air recreational facilities. It was the view of the Sports Centre manager that the combination and variety of facilities had considerably increased overall usage. The number of people using the Sports Centre had risen significantly since the completion of the Broughton High and Ascension project.

A large number of residents (approximately 5000 households in the immediate vicinity) have potentially benefited from the project. Of those interviewed the vast majority appreciated the visual improvements to the area, and over half had increased their usage of the site, either in terms of usage of the sports and recreational facilities, or as a through route, or simply as an area to sit down or walk around. The recreational facilities also attracted users from outside of the Broughton district.

However, there were some criticisms of the layout and design of the project from residents and users. A number of parents commented that more appropriate play facilities could be provided for younger children (the recreational facilities tend to cater for school children and adults). There was some demand for additional lighting, although at the same time there was a general appreciation of the costly nature of that type of improvement. In terms of landscaping and design there was praise for the use of mature trees and planting, but criticism of the positioning of footpaths which, because of the football area, are restricted to the perimeter of the site. Unfortunately the lack of footpaths on the grassed area had led to grass being worn away as users have created their own paths.

Overall, impressions of the project have been highly favourable. Officers of Salford City Council see the project as making a significant contribution to the provision of recreational facilities and environmental improvements in Salford and their views are reinforced by the positive comments made by the two schools and residents of the area.

11   The Bansteads, Leeds

Design features

- Re-use of materials – Yorkstone setts and railway sleepers – for play areas.

- Safe surfacing materials for play areas.

- Play facilities.

Beneficiaries

- School Children.

- Youth groups.

- Elderly residents of a sheltered housing project.

- Residents overlooking the scheme.

Good practice

- Public consultation.

- Responsive to diverse needs of a multi racial area.

- Involvement of school children.

- Re-use of materials in the play area.

- Successful combination of a variety of activities.

- Community involvement.

- Visual improvements will be further enhanced as the project develops.

Key facts

An amenity scheme, situated in the Harehills area of Leeds, which has provided two play areas, seating areas, an informal kickabout area, a meeting place and a school garden.

Size:		20,000 square metres.
Cost:	*Capital:*	£185,219 (1983-86).
	Revenue:	Estimated annual expenditure on maintenance £24,336.
Funding sources:		Urban Programme (capital) Leeds City Council (revenue).
Initiator:		Planning Department, Leeds City Council.
Implementation:		Leisure Services Department, Leeds City Council.

The Bansteads is situated on a two hectare City Council site within the Harehills area of Leeds. Housing clearance provided a major opportunity to improve local amenities in an area severely deficient in public open space. The primary objective was to provide a local park to meet as many local needs as possible. The original design was significantly changed after local authority consultation with the community and a revised scheme has subsequently been developed. This includes two play areas with equipment for different age groups, a garden associated with sheltered housing, an open grassed area for informal ball games, an amphitheatre that provides an informal meeting place and a school garden.

Origins

The Harehills area had suffered from blight and uncertainty dating back to the 1960's. In the mid 1970's major efforts were made to improve housing which helped to stem further decline. But until 1980 there had been no spare land for new development or new community facilities. The approval of a clearance and compulsory purchase order in June 1980 ensured the removal of several streets of substandard housing, thereby providing the opportunity for a major open space project. Deficiency of public open space and local community pressure favoured its development for amenity use rather than housing.

Design, implementation and maintenance

Leeds City Planning Department proposals envisaged that the environmental improvement scheme would be implemented immediately the site was cleared of housing and it was anticipated that the design would incorporate facilities for all age groups including a kickabout area, play equipment, together with areas of grass and tree planting. The details of design and materials were to be decided in consultation with local ward members of the Council and the local community.

These consultations resulted in the project achieving a high profile with the local community and amongst newly elected ward members. Public meetings were held and schools in the vicinity of the site were asked for comments. The local community group – Harehills Action Group – took advice from an independent landscape architect and put forward alternative proposals to those outlined by the City's Leisure Services Department. These included changes to the design content, the planting and the use of alternative materials.

Two local schools were consulted on how the open space might best meet their requirements, and they held a competition to provide a name for the park. 'The Bansteads' was the winner and duly adopted. The public consultation procedure resulted in the project brief and consequently the design and costing of the scheme being considerably changed, from the

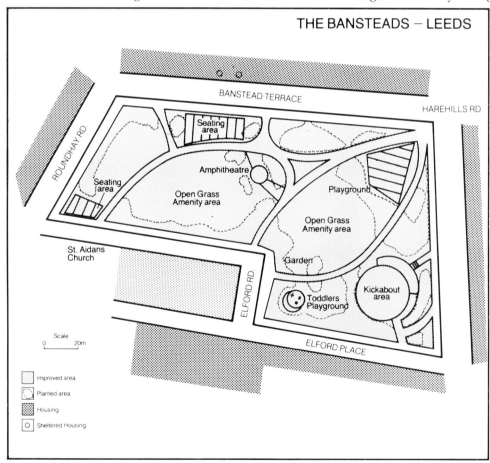

Plan 9: Bansteads Amenity Area

76

Figure 20: A walled kickabout area that is popular with the local school and youths.

Figure 21: A garden with seating has been located close to a sheltered housing development for the elderly.

original cost estimate of £120,000 with work phased over three years 1982–5, to an estimated cost of £186,300.

The redesign of the Bansteads saw the incorporation of a range of features which ensure that this park meets as many local needs as possible. There are two play areas, one for toddlers and one for older children, situated with the location of two existing major roads and a sheltered housing development in mind. The play areas are of modern construction using hardwood – sleepers and telegraph poles. Soft binding materials have been used for surface areas. A garden with seating has been located close to a sheltered housing development for the benefit of both residents and day visitors.

A graded open grassland space is intended for general amenity with a small amphitheatre built of Yorkstone setts close by. This forms the main hard landscaping feature within the Bansteads, and provides a good meeting place for local groups.

A second open grass space, suitable for ball games, is located towards the centre of the site, well away from main roads and with only a slight gradient. A walled kickabout area is popular with local youth groups and, to some extent, local schools (figure 20). A small garden area, for use by local schools, has also been included within the design. Close to the bus stops and a main pedestrian thoroughfare is a brick paved seating area (figure 21).

The project was implemented by Leeds Leisure Services Department with children from two nearby schools planting trees on the site. However, the length of implementation was of particular concern to local residents. Expectations had been raised by the consultation exercise but progress was felt to be slow. Work began in July 1983 and was completed, after only slight slippage, two years later.

Maintenance work is undertaken by Leeds Leisure Services Department. To date maintenance implications have been high due to heavy usage, some vandalism and establishing the newly planted areas.

Project schedule – The Bansteads

June 1980	Clearance Order for the Bansteads approved by Secretary of State for the Environment.
October 1980	Rehousing began.
February 1981	Planning proposals for use of the Bansteads as multipurpose open space.
September 1981	The Bansteads is included within 1982/83 IAP submission for funding to 1984/85; implementation to coincide with housing clearance.
1981/82	Consultations with local community, ward members and local schools.
October 1982	Scheme redesigned and costed; plans redrawn; clearance completed.
July 1983	Landscaping work initiated.
January 1985	Local schools invited to take part in shrub planting.
October 1985	Project works completed.

Costs

The estimated capital costs of the project total £185,219 and are itemised below:

		£
(i)	Earthworks, including soiling and drainage	48,000
(ii)	Tree Planting	15,000
(iii)	School Gardens	1,500
(iv)	Two Play Areas	23,114
(v)	Kickabout Area, including wall and terrace	22,000
(vi)	Footpaths and lighting	20,105
(vii)	Seating Areas	15,000
(viii)	Amphitheatre	20,000
(ix)	Professional Fees	20,500

Maintenance work is undertaken by the City Leisure Services Department at an estimated annual cost of £24,336.

Beneficiaries

A high level of activity at the Bansteads reflects the fact that this park was redesigned to accommodate the perceived and indicated needs of the local community. Even during the implementation phases pedestrians, dogwalkers and children (notably those with BMX bicycles) all used the site.

Although the benefits to residents overlooking the site were marginal during the implementation period the visual improvement and amenity value of the completed Bansteads is unquestionable. Most residents questioned recognised the need for a green space in an area of open space deficiency. Several felt that they were privileged to overlook a park and one resident moved into the area because the house she would occupy overlooked The Bansteads. Those residents with children recognised the benefit of close proximity to play facilities.

The sheltered housing development which opened in May 1983 has 48 residents and 250 members, 40 – 50 of whom attend the centre daily. The majority of residents are incapable of walking far so the seating area in the Bansteads provides an opportunity for them to sit outside.

Harehills Community Centre, which provides facilities for both the older and more youthful members of the community, is situated in the basement of Harehills Middle School overlooking the site. Consequently, there was obvious potential for outdoor activities once the Bansteads was completed.

Harehills Middle School has 450 pupils on the roll and nearby Harehills Primary School has 653 pupils including those attending the nursery. The children from both schools were involved in the competition to name the park and they were encouraged to assist in tree and shrub planting by the Leisure Services Department. The Middle School plan to use the 'kickabout' for small games activities, and the school gardens for ecological studies.

A very wide range of benefits have been derived by this project. The diverse needs and requirements of local people have been met and the visual improvement will be further enhanced as the planting matures.

Visual Enhancements

12 Exchange Station Car Park, Bradford

Design features

- Stonecleaning of retaining wall.
- Provision of walkways.
- Re-use of stone patio as part of the entrance.
- Tree and shrub planting.
- Rockery.

Beneficiaries

- Occupants of surrounding buildings.
- Retailers.
- Users of car park.
- The image of Bradford.

Good practice

- Effective use of remaining features of Exchange Station.
- Encouraged private sector interest in the site.
- Part of a policy to upgrade the image of Bradford city centre.
- Successful combination of facilities for motorists and pedestrians.
- Strong visual impact on prominent site.
- Meets environmental and economic objectives.

Key facts

Peripheral landscaping of a centrally situated development site and provision of a temporary car park.

Size:		21,000 square metres.
Cost:	*Capital:*	£183,000 (1980-84).
	Revenue:	Not estimated.
Funding sources:		Urban Programme (£126,000) Metropolitan Borough of Bradford (£57,000) plus revenue.
Initiator:		Planning Department, Metropolitan Borough of Bradford.
Implementation:		City Works Organisation, Metropolitan Borough of Bradford.

Vacant land is a characteristic of most inner urban areas of England. Large sites in central locations awaiting redevelopment are used in the meantime as unsightly car parks or simply boarded up. The Metropolitan Borough of Bradford, owners of a large prominent development site in the city centre, have shown that landscaping of the periphery of such sites can be beneficial. In this way the former Exchange Station has been enhanced to popular satisfaction, providing much needed extra car parking space and a landscape barrier between the development site and shop lined thoroughfares.

Origins

Exchange Station was demolished in 1976 leaving a large clearance site close to the city centre. Although the site appeared to have considerable development potential developers have been slow to act.

In order to bring the site into use proposals for the site were put forward by Bradford Planning Department in 1979. These sought to utilise part of the site for short stay parking purposes, and provided for landscaping works to be undertaken around the periphery of the site. The objectives of these proposals were threefold. Firstly, the vacant site was something of an eyesore and improvement would assist in upgrading the image of the city centre. Secondly, enhancement might attract private sector interest in the development of the site. Lastly, there was an amenity objective in relation to the shoppers and users of the car park.

Design, implementation and maintenance

It was clear that the works necessary to meet these objectives would have to be phased over a number of years. The design of the initial phases incorporated, in addition to providing much needed car parking, the removal of part of the former station retaining wall. Landscaping, which included grading, grassing, standard tree and shrub planting, improved a prominent portion of the site adjoining the car park.

A later phase provided pedestrian walkways and steps from the car park level down to Drake Street and Station Court. Associated landscaping and works to the remaining sections of the retaining wall were undertaken. These included provision and planting out of a rockery above part of the retaining wall on Drake Street and cleaning, repairing and repainting sections of the retaining wall.

Additional peripheral enhancement works were undertaken as part of the last phase of work. Banks and walls which form abutments for Bridge Street and Vicar Lane were repaired and a number of standard trees were planted in locations around the periphery

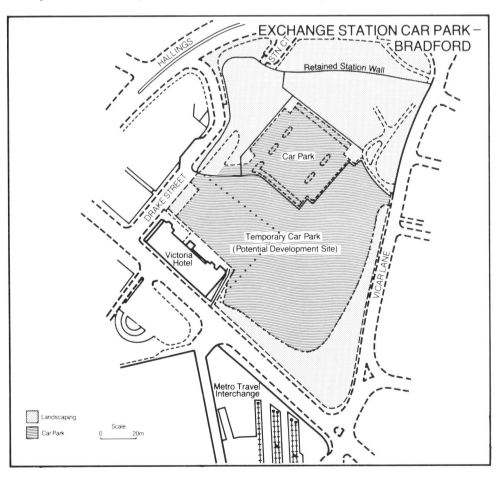

Plan 10: The layout of Exchange Station Car Park

Figure 22: A prominent stone parapet which carries steps down to street level was cleaned and repainted.

Figure 23: Landscaping the periphery of the site has provided new green space in the city centre which will be retained when development occurs.

of the site. A stone patio, formerly part of Exchange Station, was cleaned and repainted and has been used in conjunction with the steps to provide an attractive and prominent entrance to the site from Drake Street (figure 22).

Implementation of the work was undertaken by the Metropolitan Borough of Bradford City's Works Organisation. Initial works began in 1980 and were undertaken in intermittent phases with the most recent activity taking place in 1984.

Maintenance requirements include grass cutting which takes place in rotation with other environmental improvement schemes and parks in the city. Planting on the periphery of the site has been relatively successful with few natural losses. As a result this has reduced the need for replacements. Litter, however, is a particular problem which is exacerbated by the windy open aspects of the car park and the lack of litter bins. Vandalism, perhaps surprisingly for such a well used site, does not appear to be a problem.

Project schedule – Exchange Station Car Park

1976	Exchange Station demolished.
March 1980	DoE approval for car park and initial landscaping works.
1980/1	Shortstay car park opened.
1981/2	Landscaping works and removal of part of former station retaining wall.
1982/83	Pedestrian walkways, steps, cleaning and repair of retaining wall.
1983/4	Repairs to Bridge St and Vicar Lane abutments; additional planting.

Costs

The costs of the phased enhancement works are as follows:

- Implementation of a short stay car park; £42,000 (1980/81) funded from Urban Programme resources.

- Landscaping, including removal of part of the former station retaining wall; £33,000 (1981/82) funded by the Metropolitan Borough of Bradford after an unsuccessful bid for Derelict Land Grant.

- Pedestrian walkways and steps, associated landscaping, works to the former station retaining wall and parapet; £84,000 (1981-4) from Urban Programme resources and £24,000 (1982/3) from Metropolitan Borough of Bradford.

Beneficiaries

Visual enhancement has been achieved around the periphery of the site, which benefits nearby shops and passers by. Being close to the city centre the car park is particularly well used and users were unanimous that the site had been visually improved by the schemes that had been undertaken. In addition to those who have parked their cars, the site is frequently crossed by pedestrians on their way to shops and nearby bus stations.

Interest from developers for this prime city centre site has been encouraged though no agreements have yet been reached. The current high level of office vacancy and depressed rental values in the city centre may be acting as disincentives. However, by successfully raising the profile of the site it is hoped that more sustainable interest may be obtained in the future. Meanwhile, the car park serves as a functional benefit to the city of Bradford and the peripheral landscaping provides visual benefits which will be retained when development takes place on the site (figure 23). Exchange Station Car Park illustrates that the peripheral landscaping and the retention and enhancement of interesting features can markedly soften the impact of major underused city centre sites.

13   Baylis Road, Lambeth

Design features

- High quality landscaping works, including trees, bushes and mounding.

- Floodlit all weather playing surface with fencing and spectator terraces.

- Seating area.

- Dog free play area.

Beneficiaries

- Employees working in or near Waterloo.

- Motorists, cyclists and pedestrians.

- Local shopkeepers and street traders.

- Local residents.

Good practice

- Effective combination of facilities on a small site to suit a diversity of users.

- Strong visual impact on a prominent site.

- Extensive community involvement.

- Packaging a diversity of funding.

- Meets environmental and recreational objectives.

Key facts

The creation of a new area of public open space with recreational facilities. Located on a prominent site in Waterloo that was formerly a coach and car park.

Size:		5,000 square metres.
Cost:	*Capital:*	£383,000 1979-83.
	Revenue:	Not estimated on a project basis.
Funding sources:		Urban Programme £356,000 (1979–1983) London Borough of Lambeth. Directorate of Amenity Services, Main Programme £7,000 and revenue funding Sports Council £20,000
Initiator:		Waterloo Action Group and Department of Amenity Services, London Borough of Lambeth.
Implementation:		Department of Amenity Services, London Borough of Lambeth with assistance from the Waterloo Action Group.

The Baylis Road public open space is a small site in a prominent location in the Waterloo district of Lambeth. It offers a wide variety of amenities to suit a large cross section of the public. This is achieved despite the constraints of space. It is also of interest since the improvements to the site were initiated by a local community group who have subsequently retained an involvement, and because the imaginative and high quality design is appropriate to its prominent and busy location.

Origins

The site is a former car park and coach park, which was owned by the GLC, near the junction of Baylis Road and Waterloo Road. Waterloo Station and the South Bank arts complex are close by and The Old Vic theatre lies opposite the site in Waterloo Road.

Although there is a substantial amount of high density public housing in the vicinity of Baylis Road the main land uses are commercial. The area is an employment centre and a through route to central London (figure 24). There are high levels of vehicular and pedestrian movement nearby. The prominence of the Baylis Road site and the unsightly impact on the local environment of a car and coach park, surrounded by corrugated iron fencing, was a major factor in influencing the London Borough of Lambeth to negotiate with the GLC for purchase of the site. The second major factor was the general deficiency of either landscaping, open space or play and recreational facilities in Waterloo. The Baylis Road site offered an opportunity to develop an amenity to suit a number of user groups with a design appropriate to its prominent location.

Although the Directorate of Amenity Services of the London Borough of Lambeth had a clear rationale to develop the site the project may not have got off the ground without the presence of the Waterloo Action Group, a local community and pressure group, based in Baylis Road. It was the Waterloo Action Group which first drafted a plan for the Baylis Road site in 1978, whilst it was still in use as a car and coach park. The plan was submitted to the Directorate of Amenity Services who, with amendments, agreed to take on the project.

There then followed a lengthy period of negotiation between the London Borough of Lambeth and the Greater London Council with purchase finally being agreed in 1979. Work on the site was undertaken in two phases starting in 1981.

Design, implementation and maintenance

The design for the Baylis Road site incorporates four main features.

1. An all weather floodlit ball games area enclosed by a wall and high fence. The area is mainly used for organised five a side football. A high quality surface has been used to cater for heavy usage (figure 25).

2. A variety of seating is provided throughout the site.

3. A fenced 'dog free' play area for younger children has been incorporated, in line with the Directorate of Amenities Services' policy.

4. The remainder of the site has been given over to soft landscaping. Mounding has been provided, partly to reduce the likelihood of ball games on the grassed area and partly to enhance the design of the site. Planting has comprised bushes and standard and semi-mature trees and has been concentrated on the perimeter of the site. Given the prominent location of the site the planting is designed to provide a strong visual impact.

The initial phase of the work was undertaken in

Figure 24: Planting close to the road has visually softened and improved this busy approach to central London.

Figure 25: The Sports Council grant aided this all-weather ball games area.

1981 on the southern half of the site on the section bordered by Waterloo Road and Coral Street. This included most of the landscaping works, the seating areas and the play area. The design was prepared by the Directorate of Amenity Services after consultation with the Waterloo Action Group. The work itself was undertaken by private contractors.

The second phase of the work necessitated the closure of part of Coral Street to take the site up to the junction of Baylis Road and Waterloo Road. This addition to the site was required for the all weather, floodlit ball games area and terracing for spectators. This phase of the work was completed in 1983, later than originally hoped, because of the statutory procedures required to close the road and remove parking meters and because of problems of re-routing and removing the gas supply piping below the surface. As with the first phase the work was undertaken by a private contractor. Since completion the fence separating the ball games area from Waterloo Road has been increased in height to reduce the risk of balls being kicked out onto the main road.

Although the Waterloo Action Group try to keep a watchful eye on the site the Directorate of Amenity Services have responsibility for maintenance. There have been incidents of vandalism, particularly to the children's play area, the seating areas and the trees. Overall the planting has been reasonably successful with the exception of the heavily used areas near the seating.

Project schedule – Baylis Road

1978	Waterloo Action Group drafts a recreation and landscaping plan for the Baylis Road coach and car park. Plan submitted to the Directorate of Amenity Services, Lambeth BC.
1979	Lambeth BC agree on purchase of site with GLC. Urban Programme approval sought for project.
1981	Phase 1. Improvements made to part of the site. Landscaping works implemented.
1982–3	Road closure allowed Phase 2 to be implemented which included an all weather, ball games area.

Costs

A high proportion of the cost of this scheme is accounted for by land purchase. The purchase price from the GLC was £250,000 funded by the Urban

Programme in 1979. The Sports Council provided a £20,000 grant towards the construction cost of the all weather ball games area and London Borough of Lambeth contributed £7,000 from their main programme budgets towards basic site works. The remaining finance, £106,000, was funded from the Urban Programme and covered the landscaping and site works and the balance of the work required for the floodlit all weather ball games area.

Beneficiaries

The Waterloo Action Group are pleased that improvements on the site have gone ahead and to a design close to their original proposals. It was felt the work had been implemented to a high standard and overall the site was improving with maturity.

There was however, concern within the Action Group at the lack of permanent supervision on the site, and the incidences of vandalism. It was also thought that the ball games area could be better used, but that this may occur with organisation and experience.

Local residents were strongly appreciative of the visual improvement and were particularly impressed by the quality and diversity of the project. Office workers in the area appreciated the new amenity, welcoming an open space that can be used in summer lunchtimes (figure 26). Local businesses were generally supportive with the only reservation being the reduction in land available for nearby car and coach parking. Other beneficiaries include pedestrians, cyclists, motorists and bus passengers, who can all now enjoy the visual improvement brought about by the project.

Figure 26: A seating area within the confines of the open space.

14   Noble's Quay/Fish Quay, Sunderland

Design features

- Simple, cost effective improvements to Fish Quay.
- Street furniture in keeping with a quayside location.
- Soft landscaping – grading, grassing and planting.
- Use of attractive bricks for road and pathway at Noble's Quay.

Beneficiaries

- Fishermen and dockworkers.
- Local residents.
- Visitors to the city.

Good practice

- Improved the operational efficiency of Fish Quay.
- Part of a programme of riverside environmental improvements.
- Strong co-ordination between departments and local authorities.
- Major visual improvement.
- Meets environmental and economic objectives.

Key facts

The improvement of the operational conditions and appearance of Fish Quay, reclamation of semi-derelict Noble's Quay and subsequent development as public open space for local residents and dock workers.

Size:		5,000 square metres.
Cost:	*Capital:*	£143,000.
	Revenue:	Estimated expenditure required per annum £1,500. Actual expenditure 1985/6 £218.
Funding sources:		Urban Programme (capital) Borough of Sunderland (revenue).
Initiator:		Department of Planning, Borough of Sunderland.
Implementation:		Department of Works, Borough of Sunderland in co-ordination with Highways Department, Tyne and Wear County Council.

The potential of waterside sites for recreation and amenity use is clear, but this potential can only gradually be realised in a town such as Sunderland which has extensive areas of riverside dereliction. Considerable efforts have been required to reduce the scale of the problem by reclaiming sites. The improvement of Noble's Quay and Fish Quay, situated beside the River Wear and within a kilometer of the city centre, illustrates how economic, environmental and amenity objectives can be simultaneously addressed.

Origins

In 1978, Noble's Quay was semi derelict, Custom House Quay was unused and the quaysides were crumbling (figure 27). Fish Quay was still very much in use but operational conditions were poor and the ramshackle garage units, used by fishermen for storing their gear, were in disrepair.

'A Plan for the Riverside' produced by the Borough of Sunderland Planning Department outlined policies and proposals for the River Wear corridor and included proposals for the improvement of Noble's Quay, Custom House Quay and Fish Quay. Although the regeneration of other riverside sites was considered to have higher overall priority it was envisaged that environmental improvements here would

Figure 27: In 1978 Noble's Quay was semi-derelict, rarely used, and the quayside was crumbling.

complement works to be undertaken within the adjoining Pann's Bank Industrial Improvement Area.

Local councillors were keen to bring the project forward as they wished to see physical improvements to this section of the riverside, which is close to housing and industry and which would provide new amenities in an area in need of them.

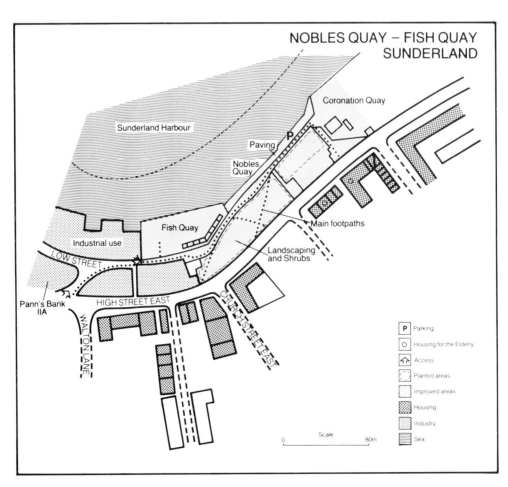

Plan 11: Noble's and Fish Quay improvements.

Design, implementation and maintenance

Clearly stated objectives lay behind the design of improvements to Noble's Quay. These incorporated the operational access requirements of adjoining Corporation Quay whilst providing an amenity space for dockers, townspeople and local residents. The crumbling quaysides of Noble's Quay and Custom House Quay were replaced and provided with new copings and black painted cast iron handrailings. They are practical and blend in well with the surroundings. Hard landscaping of the quay provides the most notable features with attractive marigold road bricks used for the roadway and red roadbricks for the quayside footpaths.

An old custom house was demolished along with walls and hoardings. The slopes on which these had stood were graded and grassed (figure 28). Other slopes that had been previously treated were enhanced by the provision of tarmac pathways and sensibly situated seating with views over the River Wear.

Dual objectives lay behind the enhancement of Fish Quay. These were to improve both the operational conditions and appearance of the quay. The achievement of these objectives required simple practical measures. Minor repairs and painting of the existing fishermen's stores has given them a new lease of life. New stores have been built, access has been improved and the lighting made more effective. These improvements have ensured that the image of Fish Quay has been brightened and that operational efficiency has been improved.

The reconstruction of the roadway into Corporation Quay which took place in 1980 and 1981 was undertaken by the Highways Department of Tyne and Wear Metropolitan County Council and funded from the Urban Programme as part of the Council's Economic Development Programme. Other works on both Noble's Quay, Fish Quay and Custom House Quay

were undertaken by the Department of Works, Borough of Sunderland. Tree and shrub planting took place in the autumn of 1981 but, due to vandalism, some replacement and additional planting had to be undertaken during the following year.

Revenue requirements of the project are estimated to be £1,500 per annum. However, so far, insufficient resources have been made available. Indeed, although only a few years have elapsed since the scheme was undertaken the high quality image of Noble's Quay has been partially lost. Grass has begun to grow between the paving blocks and the paint is peeling from the cast iron railings. Actual expenditure on maintenance in 1985/6 was only £218. The appearance of Nobles Quay in the summer of 1986 suggests this was insufficient.

Project schedule – Noble's Quay/Fish Quay

November 1978   A Plan for the Riverside: Draft Policies and Proposals published.

1979/80   Project included in approved submission.

November 1979   Work began.

1981   Basic work completed.

1981/2   Planting and minor additional works.

1982/3   Replanting and additional tree planting.

February 1984   Project completed.

Costs

The capital costs are as follows:

- Building of new fisherman's stores and improvements to Fish Quay – £52,100 (1979/80)

- Improvements to Nobles Quay – £79,900 (1980/81)

- Planting of slopes to the rear of Nobles Quay – £4,700 (1981/2)

- Replacement of planting due to vandalism and additional minor works – £6,300 (1982/3)

Figure 28: Standard treeplanting on the slopes overlooking Noble's Quay.

Beneficiaries

The main users of Fish Quay are the fishermen, who tie up their boats at the quayside to offload their catches, and stallholders, who sell fish on the quay attracting people from the town centre. The image of the quay has been enhanced and the commercial operations of the fishermen have benefited from the building repairs. Vandalism has been reduced recently as a consequence of the improved lighting but the problem still remains.

On Noble's Quay the seating provides a resting place for elderly residents from the nearby old people's home. Other local residents, particularly the less mobile elderly, enjoy the visual improvements. Dockworkers based in the vicinity of Noble's Quay also make use of the site, particularly at lunchtimes. However, not all visitors to the site are local. A number of those interviewed had travelled to Sunderland either to shop or on business and had taken time to enjoy the prospect Noble's Quay now offers.

Projects in Industrial and Commercial Areas

15 Derwenthaugh Riverside Park, Gateshead

Design features

- Improvements to existing pathway.
- Creation of new pathway.
- Construction of a riverside bank and wall.
- Creation of an island in the river.
- Construction of a weir to control river flow.
- Landscaping.

Beneficiaries

- Local residents.
- Local and potential inmoving firms.
- Visitors to Gateshead Metro Centre.

Good practices

- Good use made of the potential offered by the river.
- Helped to encourage private sector interest.
- Integral part of improvements undertaken in the Derwenthaugh IIA.
- Successful planting regime.
- Strong visual impact.
- Meets environmental and economic objectives.

Key facts

The improvement and construction of landscaped pathways along the River Derwent, undertaken as part of the changes made within Derwenthaugh Industrial Improvement Area.

Size: Length of footpath is approximately 2 km.

Cost: *Capital:* £835,000.

Revenue: Maintenance currently the responsibility of contractors.

Funding sources: Department of the Environment, allocation for Derwenthaugh IIA. Total expenditure to date is £3.199m.

Initiator: Planning Department, Gateshead MBC.

Implementation: Planning Department, Gateshead MBC and private contractors.

The river Derwent is a tributary of the River Tyne, the confluence of the two rivers lies approximately four kilometres from the centre of Gateshead. The area surrounding the river Derwent is known as Derwenthaugh, an area once characterised by dereliction and still including a power station, a coal washing plant and railway sidings, the hallmarks of a passing industrial era. The river Derwent itself was heavily polluted and steered a course through some of the ugliest parts of Derwenthaugh (figure 29).

Figure 29: The middle section of the river prior to work being undertaken.

In order to help revive Derwenthaugh as a place to live and work and to improve its appearance Gateshead Metropolitan Borough Council declared the area an Industrial Improvement Area (IIA). One of the projects arising from the IIA was the creation of a riverside park and pathway along a two kilometres stretch of the River Derwent. This project has led to the radical transformation of the appearance of the river and its surrounding environment. The project also realised the potential of the river as a natural feature to provide an amenity for local residents and visitors to the area and has, as part of wider environmental improvements in Derwenthaugh IIA, helped to improve the image and increase the investment potential of this part of Gateshead (figure 30).

Origins

The riverside park and pathway was first mooted in the Dunston and Swalwell Riverside District Plan prepared by Gateshead MBC Planning Department in 1978. This plan placed great emphasis on the need to improve the physical environment of Derwenthaugh.

The opportunity to transform the area around the River Derwent arose with the declaration of the Derwenthaugh IIA, covering 100 hectares, in 1979. The scale of dereliction and the poor road access to the area made Derwenthaugh a logical choice for an IIA.

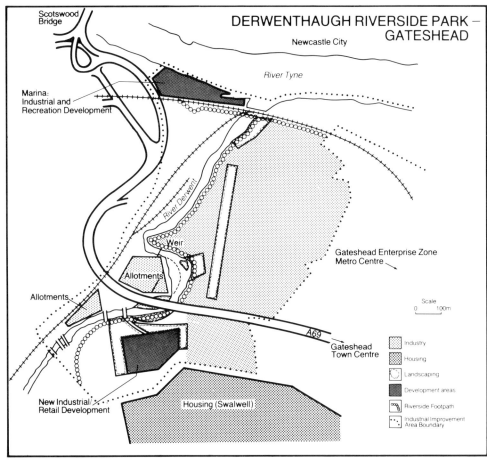

Plan 12: Derwenthaugh Riverside Park.

Figure 30: The mudflats have been removed and an island created as a nature reserve.

Figure 31: The park at its narrowest with access to the river for water sports

The Derwenthaugh IIA complements the infrastructure improvements which have and which are being made to the western area of Gateshead. A new bypass, part of which crosses the IIA and the Riverside Park, takes the A69 from Gateshead to Scotswood Bridge and towards the north, significantly improving access to what has traditionally been an isolated district of Gateshead. In addition, land to the east of the IIA was declared an Enterprise Zone. A key feature of the Zone is the construction of the Gateshead Metro Centre, now partially open, which when completed will be one of Britain's largest 'out of town' retail and leisure centres.

Design, implementation and maintenance

Whilst the objective has been to landscape and improve the visual appearance throughout the IIA, the area in the vicinity of the River Derwent offered Gateshead MBC Planning Department, the best opportunity to make a noticeable visual impact.

Gateshead Planning Department were able, because of the funding available due to IIA status, to improve the stretch of the river between the Tyne and a residential area known as Swalwell, adjacent to Derwenthaugh. Overall the project covers a 2 km stretch of the River Derwent.

The design for the Riverside Park proposed both improvements to existing and new pathways, improvements to the river and improvements to the area in the immediate vicinity of the river.

A pathway has been constructed along the eastern bank of the River Derwent making use of previously existing sections of pathways which provided access for local residents to allotments. These old pathways were overgrown and have been tidied up, relaid with stone chippings, and landscaped to blend with the entirely new sections.

The new and refurbished pathway has been linked

to improvements to the river flow. A new, vertical concrete bank has been constructed. This improves the flow of the river and decreases the likelihood of silting, which was a major problem prior to the construction of the bank. In addition, it allows the footpath to now follow the course of the river. The new bank has an attractive brightly coloured railing. However, there is a two metre drop to the river and the wide spacing between horizontal railings might be considered insecure for young children. As part of the work a weir has been constructed. This weir, together with reclamation work, has reduced tidal movement and an island has been created in the river, which has been planted to provide a natural habitat. Pollution levels have been reduced by the improved flow in the river and allow some fishing. However, the nearby coal washing plant further upstream still adversely affects water quality. Steps have been provided in the river bank to facilitate usage for boating and canoeing (figure 31), but as yet the river has not been used for this purpose.

The length of the pathway has been landscaped with semi-mature and standard trees, bushes and grassed areas. There is, however, only limited space available adjacent to the pathway. In some sections the pathway is too close to industrial buildings to allow anything other than a few bushes or individual trees. Elsewhere there is space for extensive grassed areas, densely planted areas of trees and shrubs and additional pathways leading away from the river. For example, in the middle section of the park the landscaped area stretches 20 to 30 metres away from the river.

General environmental improvements also include the resiting and improvement of allotments, grant aided landscaping improvements to the adjacent radio station car park, the development of new attractively designed small industrial units and a D.I.Y centre. An inscribed stone located in the middle of the park serves both as a landmark and provides the park with a focal point. As yet little, apart from land purchase, has been done to improve the environment of the western bank of the River Derwent. The long term plans of the Planning Department are to extend the landscaping works to this area.

The work was undertaken between 1979 and 1985. Work was undertaken in stages commencing in the southern part of the IIA and finishing close to the Tyne. Design was the responsibility of Gateshead Planning Department, which was assisted by other departments, most notably the Engineering Department. The bulk of the work was contracted out to specialist firms who also have responsibility for initial maintenance. Maintenance work for the landscaping aspects of the site will gradually become the responsibility of the Gateshead Council's Parks Department.

Project schedule – Derwenthaugh Riverside Park

1978	Riverside Park proposed in Dunston and Swalwell Riverside District Plan, Gateshead MBC.
1979	Declaration of Derwenthaugh IIA. Work started on designing Riverside Park.
1979–1985	Implementation of Riverside Park project undertaken in stages starting with the southernmost section. Declaration of Gateshead Enterprise Zone and the construction of the Metro Centre.

Costs

The development of the Riverside Park has been funded from the allocation for Derwenthaugh Industrial Improvement Area which, to date, totals over £3 million. A total of £1.2 million has been spent on improving the environment of Derwenthaugh and the majority of these resources have been directed towards the Riverside park. The capital cost of the Riverside Park was £835,000 which includes the following items:

- The construction of the riverwall and the weir   £663,000

- Improvements to the river bank including the footpath and landscaping works   £121,000

- The relocation of and improvements to the allotments   £51,000

All items are at historic cost prices.

Beneficiaries

A number of enterprises located in the Derwenthaugh IIA were interviewed as part of a study of industrial and commercial improvement areas. In general existing industry within the IIA attached relatively little importance to the improvements undertaken. Indeed 80% of those interviewed attached no importance to the physical environment. However, the improvements were not primarily designed for the existing, predominantly heavy industrial, enterprises located in the IIA but more for potential in-moving industry. Even so several employers cited the development of the Riverside Park as a reason for staying in Derwenthaugh.

The Riverside Park located approximately 1 km from the Metro Centre is probably too distant to influence location decisions on that site. However, the park has contributed to the overall environmental and infrastructural change in Derwenthaugh which, in turn, has been a factor in the development of the Metro Centre. Closer at hand the D.I.Y. centre which adjoins the Riverside Park is set to expand, demonstrating confidence in the area.

Local residents, when consulted in the above mentioned study, were generally enthusiastic about the riverside park. Although the housing area fell outside the IIA, all of the residents were aware of the development of the Riverside Park. The vast majority of residents welcomed the project and saw it as a substantial visual and recreational improvement. Many residents (66%) used the recreational facilities in the area, particularly the riverside walks and allotments. The creation of the Riverside Park was given as a reason for increased usage. Indeed, the riverside walks had attracted visitors from outside the immediate area.

Criticisms of the project were less concerned with what had been done but what still remained. Residents pointed to the continued, albeit reduced, levels of water pollution and the overall environment of Derwenthaugh which is still, to some extent, characterised by dereliction and heavy industry. The Riverside Park has been an important attempt to remedy the environmental problems of Derwenthaugh but residents, employers and the local authority are well aware of the scale of work that still needs to be undertaken.

16   Trencherfield Mill, Wigan

Design features

- Dense planting for immediate visual impact.
- High quality hard landscaping works.
- Information boards.
- Items associated with the industrial past.
- Raised flower beds.

Beneficiaries

- Employees at Trencherfield Mill.
- Visitors to the exhibition areas on the ground floor.
- Visitors to other facilities in the Wigan Pier improvement scheme
- Courtaulds.

Good practice

- Good use of mill buildings and surrounding area.
- Retained and helped increase local employment opportunities.
- Linked to wider objectives of Wigan Pier project.
- Co-ordinated approach between local authority departments.
- Successful planting regime.
- Low maintenance requirements.
- Strong visual impact.
- Meets economic, environmental and recreational objectives.

Key facts

Peripheral landscaping of a car park on the site of a formerly derelict piece of land adjacent to a cotton mill. Situated in the industrial core of Wigan, Trencherfield Mill has been established as a visitor facility for heritage, concert hall and technical college activities. The mill is an integral part of the Wigan Pier development.

Size:		5,000 square metres.
Cost:	*Capital:*	£42,000 (1982/3).
	Revenue:	Estimated expenditure on maintenance £4,000 for first 3 years; £2,000 subsequently.
Funding sources:		Urban Programme (capital). Wigan Metropolitan Borough Council (revenue).
Initiator:		Department of Technical Services, Wigan Metropolitan Borough Council.
Implementation:		Department of Leisure Services, Wigan Metropolitan Borough Council. Private contractors.

Making the most of industrial heritage has become increasingly important in the regeneration of many local economies. The visual improvement of buildings, the location of new amenities in rundown historic industrial core areas and the establishment of heritage centres and museums have all or some of the following aims:

- attraction of visitors
- improvement of the living and working environment
- improvement of the image of an area
- encouragement of business confidence in an area.

By pursuing these aims it is hoped that the service sector may propser and that existing manufacturing industry may be retained.

Wigan Metropolitan Borough Council have undertaken environmental improvements as an integral part of their economic regeneration initiatives. Trees have been planted throughout the Borough, and the historic industrial area around Wigan Pier has become a show piece, heritage scheme. Trencherfield Mill was one of the canalside buildings which offered some potential for restoration, a potential that has now been realised. Employment retention has been associated with the restoration works, facility provision and high quality landscaping. The latter ensures an immediate visual impact on visitors and contributes to the other benefits derived from the project.

Origins

Wigan MBC has placed emphasis upon retaining and supporting industry in the Borough. This has been achieved through access improvements, provision of premises and environmental improvement.

When Courtaulds enquired about planning permission to build a superstore on their Trencherfield Mill site in 1981 the prospect of the loss of 130 manufacturing jobs prompted the council to intervene. Wigan MBC purchased Trencherfield Mill, after reaching the agreement that all the jobs were to be retained using the four upper floors of the mill, and with Courtaulds remaining as tenants. The ground floor will be used for exhibition space, an educational area and an industrial museum, together forming a part of the development of Wigan Pier as a major tourism project.

It was anticipated that there would be intense pressure on car parking space. The purchase of Trencherfield Mill provided the opportunity for a new parking area which would serve both visitors to the heritage centre and employees working in the Mill.

Design and implementation

The main features adjacent to Trencherfield Mill were a part filled mill reservoir and derelict land (figure 32). Urban Programme funding was used to transform this formerly derelict area into a car park. The design for a subsequent phase of the work will comprehensively landscape the car park perimeter. The need to create a favourable impression on visitors led to the specification of high quality landscaping, designed to be attractive from the outset.

Reclamation work took place during 1982 and the peripheral landscaping was undertaken in the spring of 1983. The desired visual image has been achieved in a variety of ways.

Dense shrub planting has ensured good ground cover, together with paving and raised flower beds constructed of red brick, blend with the cleaned brick of Trencherfield Mill (figure 33). The raised flower beds also offer protection to the planted areas. Attention to detail includes the design of lamposts using distinctive spherical lamps. All of this gives the site a modern 'feel' whilst retaining features of 'old' Wigan Pier. These include a five metre high, floodlit steamhammer and a canal barge on the grassed areas between the car park, the Mill and the nearby canal. A colliery fan will be added as an additional feature.

The Department of Technical Services of Wigan

Figure 32: The part filled mill reservoir and derelict land prior to improvement.

Figure 33: Paving and raised flower beds blend with cleaned brick at the Mill entrance.

Figure 34: Information and direction signs in the car park steers visitors to the attractions.

MBC took the lead in pursuing the Trencherfield Mill scheme and have co-ordinated closely with a number of other Departments, including Education and Leisure Services. The landscaping works were undertaken by private contractors working to the design and specification of the Leisure Services Department (figure 34).

Project schedule – Trencherfield Mill

1981   Threatened closure at Trencherfield Mill.

1982   Reclamation of part filled mill reservoir and derelict land.

Spring 1983   Peripheral landscaping works undertaken.

Costs
The capital cost of the landscaping works, which included the importation of topsoil, totalled £42,000. Revenue implications of the project reflect the need to maintain a high quality of presentation. These have been estimated to be £4,000 per annum for the first three years, to include replacement planting, falling to £2,000 in subsequent years.

Beneficiaries
The exhibition area and industrial museum are attracting large numbers of visitors and the educational area is visited by many student groups. All those using the building – employees, visitors, students, teachers – derive visual benefits from the quality and convenience of the car park. Easy access to the other facilities of the Wigan Pier ensures that the car park is well used at all times; Wigan Civic Trust commented that the car park 'must be one of the most attractive and welcoming in the country'.

Courtaulds have also derived considerable benefits from the Trencherfield Mill project through improved access, parking and above all the immediate working environment. The Council's commitment to the improvements also encouraged Courtaulds to remain in Wigan. Otherwise 130 jobs would probably have been lost to the town. Indeed the employment of the Mill has actually increased by approximately 200 people.

17 Electric Avenue, Lambeth

Design features

- Reverse camber, concrete block carriageway running flush with paved walkway.

- Cast iron 'cannon' shaped bollards.

- Environmental works undertaken on buildings in Electric Avenue.

Beneficiaries

- Pedestrians.

- Shoppers.

- Street traders.

- Building owners.

- Shopkeepers.

Good practice

- Responded to the needs of traders and shopkeepers.

- Improved the image of Brixton as a commercial area.

- Linked to strategy to revive Brixton town centre.

- Good co-ordination between departments to get the project underway.

- Low additional maintenance requirements.

- Private sector contribution to project costs.

Key facts

The refurbishment of a run down shopping street in central Brixton. Building facades have been cleaned and the road resurfaced and improved.

Size:	24,000 square metres.
Cost: Capital:	£167,500 (1981–3) Cost of repaving works. £104,000 (1984–86) Cleaning and repair of building facades.
Revenue:	Negligible revenue effect.
Funding sources:	Urban Programme. Private Sector (25% of cleaning and repair of building facades).
Initiator:	Directorate of Town Planning, London Borough of Lambeth. Directorate of Civil Engineering and Public Services, London Borough of Lambeth. Directorate of Environmental Health, London Borough of Lambeth.
Implementation:	Private Contractors under guidance from the Directorate of Civil Engineering and Public Services, London Borough of Lambeth.

Repaving and associated environmental improvements along Electric Avenue in the centre of Brixton show how confidence can be restored to an urban shopping street.

Origins

A repaving scheme on Electric Avenue had long been considered by the London Borough of Lambeth as having the potential to play a significant role in reviving Brixton Town Centre (figure 35). A Draft Action Area Plan stressed that to ensure Brixton's future as a 'strategic centre' and to continue to provide local residents with a full range of shops, leisure and cultural facilities, it was necessary to improve the quality of the environment and conditions for pedestrians. The proposals for improving Electric Avenue were drawn up following consultations between the Directorates of Town Planning, Environmental Health and Consumer Services of the London Borough of Lambeth.

At the hub of pedestrian movement throughout the shopping centre, Electric Avenue had the advantage of lying off the main road network. The opportunity was there to create a paved precinct where pedestrians might enjoy some priority over vehicles, without impeding the operation of an existing street market. In addition to paving, Lambeth BC proposed to restore a canopy which had been partially removed several years before. However, in view of the high cost of the canopy restoration, this aspect of the scheme was deferred in favour of completely repaving Electric Avenue. The proposal to repave Electric Avenue was discussed with street market traders at a meeting held in October 1981. They recognised that there would be benefits for both shoppers and themselves and approved the scheme subject to detailed consultations on phasing and temporary relocation before work began.

Design, implementation and maintenance

Both phases of the resurfacing involved deep excavation of the existing road to accommodate a change in its cross-section. Traditional surfaces with camber from centre down to kerb were replaced by concrete carriageway blocks, with a shallow rider to act as a sewer in the middle. This was primarily of value to market traders, but pedestrians also benefited for the carriageway blocks were constructed flush with the renewed pavement slabs to create a continuity between the carriageway and pavement. Cast iron cannon-shaped bollards have been positioned between the footpath and carriageway as statutory closure of the road has been opposed on grounds of access.

Repaving work was undertaken in two phases. The first phase used an underspend on capital budget allocations which effectively brought the project forward. Having the scheme approved enabled the allocation to be taken up and work begun within the same financial year. Indeed, further funds were taken up that year by the pre-purchase of materials in advance of the second phase. Both phases involved the resurfacing of the roadway and pavement of Electric Avenue. This work was completed by December 1982. Private sector contractors undertook the implementation of the scheme under the supervision of the Directorate of Civil Engineering and Public Services.

Apart from repaving work a number of other improvements have been made. Parts of the original wrought iron canopy have been removed, brickwork and facades have been cleaned, masonry treated, windows repaired and, in some cases, replaced (figure 36). Plans have been drawn up for the replication of the canopy in light-weight materials. This aspect of the improvements has been programmed for September 1986 and will be completed in June 1987.

Figure 35: Before improvement, Electric Avenue, at the heart of the town centre, had the potential to play a significant role in the revival of Brixton's town centre.

Figure 36: Shopkeepers, traders and shoppers now enjoy better access and improved image.

Project schedule – Electric Avenue

May 1980	Brixton Town Centre Draft Action Area Plan published; pedestrianisation of Electric Avenue proposed.
July 1980	Town Planning Committee approval gained for scheme to repave and reinstate canopy on Electric Avenue.
October 1980	Policy and Resources Committee advised that the projects should not proceed until finance available.
October 1981	Repaving proposal discussed with street traders.
December 1981	Repaving of Electric Avenue included in the Lambeth Inner City Partnership's Environmental Improvement Package for 1981/2.
Feb.-March 1982	Phase I of repaving undertaken.
March 1982	Prepurchase of materials for second phase of work sanctioned by Public Services Sub Committee.
Aug. to Dec. 1982	Phase II implemented.
March to October 1984	Facades of building on Electric Avenue cleaned and repainted.
February to June 1985	Facades on the side of Electric Avenue cleaned
September 1986 – June 1987	Canopy to be reinstated.

Costs

Resurfacing Electric Avenue involved considerable excavation works, high cost materials and restricted hours of access which led to high labour costs. Nevertheless, the scheme was implemented for less than the estimated cost. The detailed costs are as follows:

Site clearance and excavation	23,700	14%
Drainage	20,200	12%
Paving (Footway)	31,700	19%
(Carriageway)	35,600	21%
Bollards	10,500	6%
– erect and paint	4,800	3%
Restricted working on cost	35,400	21%
Engineers Fees	4,300	3%
Road closure & Other studies	1,300	1%
TOTAL	£167,500	100%

Facade cleaning and repair works were funded through the powers offered by the Commercial Improvement Area status of Electric Avenue at a cost of £104,000. The building owners contributed 25% of these costs. The cleansing of the street market in Electric Avenue has a service cost of about £50,000 per annum but the level of service has not altered since the repaving so there is no revenue effect implied. However, the block paving is known to be a little more difficult to cleanse thoroughly.

Beneficiaries

Discussions with shopkeepers and street-traders on Electric Avenue revealed that the improvements had increased their confidence in the area. Changes in investment, employment and turnover have been marginal and not obviously related to the improvements. Nevertheless, shopkeepers and traders saw the benefits of the works in terms of improved image, better access and visual enhancement. Many looked forward to the erection of the canopy which could attract passing trade and provide cover for the market stalls in bad weather.

Unfortunately, when the London Borough of Lambeth was unable to secure a statutory closure order on Electric Avenue from the GLC, as highways authority, access was only restricted to 'permitted' vehicles so congestion is sometimes a problem. The cannon shaped bollards do, however, retain pedestrian priority on the pavements. Although not as originally conceived, the free passage of shoppers in this busy market street has been encouraged.

Improvements to Electric Avenue have restored confidence in a rundown shopping street and together with other improvements being undertaken in the vicinity, including those to nearby British Rail property, central Brixton is becoming a more pleasant place to live, work and shop.

18 Bexley Square, Salford

Design features

- High quality hard landscaping with planting of semi-mature trees.

- Use of 'period' style cast iron bollards and lamposts.

- Provision of seating and signposting.

Beneficiaries

- Residents and employees of Salford.

- Local businesses.

- Passing traffic.

Good practice

- Designed to complement surrounding buildings.

- Improved the confidence of local businesses.

- Linked to IIA and conservation area policies and to a programme of environmental improvement works along the A6.

- Low maintenance requirements.

- Strong visual impacts.

- Further improvements planned.

Key facts

Pedestrianisation of part of Bexley Square, Salford. Landscaping of the site and the provision of amenities.

Size:		125 square metres.
Cost:	Capital:	£38,000 1983/4.
	Revenue:	General maintenance undertaken. No specific cost estimates.
Funding sources:		Urban Programme (capital). Salford City Council (revenue).
Initiator:		Planning Department, Salford MBC.
Implementation:		Planning Department and Direct Works Department, Salford MBC.

Bexley Square is located within the Chapel Street Industrial Improvement Area, Salford. It also forms part of a conservation area. The square is bounded on two sides by shops, offices and a public house. On a third side stands the old Salford Town Hall (a building of considerable local interest) and on the fourth the A6 (Chapel Street), a major route into Salford. Prior to pedestrianisation work being undertaken there was direct access from Bexley Square onto the A6.

The works undertaken in Bexley Square are of high quality and have used materials sympathetic to the existing environment, notably Salford Town Hall and the buildings adjacent to the square. The project provides a quiet and secluded rest area which has become popular amongst local residents and employees. The project is also part of a wider programme of improvements both in the IIA and along the A6 corridor and the project has been influential in the encouraging of private sector investment, particularly amongst the employers within Bexley Square, who have undertaken grant aided environmental improvement works.

Origins

Environmental improvements undertaken in Bexley Square and elsewhere along the A6 originated from a policy document prepared by Salford's deputy Chief Executive in 1980. That document highlighted the importance of the A6, as a major arterial route, to the overall image of Salford. It also noted the potential for undertaking environmental works given the concentrations of historic buildings along or in the vicinity of the A6.

The resultant policy was the promotion and undertaking of improvement works, mainly to buildings using Urban Programme resources, within an 'environmental improvement corridor' extending approximately two kilometres along the A6. These works were to be complemented by the expenditure made within Chapel Street IIA and the creation of a walkway along the River Irwell.

For Bexley Square it was proposed that partial pedestrianisation should be undertaken and that the frontages of buildings should be improved where appropriate.

Design, implementation and maintenance

It was decided from the outset that the part of Bexley Square directly in front of the Town Hall, adjoining Browning Street, would be left as it was to enable traffic to turn and to provide access for supply vehicles to the public house and shops. The remainder of the square (approximately 125 sq m) would be closed to traffic and paved for pedestrian usage and, as a result, vehicular access to the A6 (Chapel Street) would be denied.

The landscaping undertaken in Bexley Square has had to take into consideration its status as a conservation area. Therefore, cast iron as opposed to concrete bollards have been used where the pedestrianised area meets the road, and Victorian style lamposts have been set into the paved area (figure 37).

A mixture of concrete and brick paving has been used for the surface within which tall standard and semi mature trees have been planted. In the centre of the pedestrianised area and at the Chapel Street entrance to the Square seating, using wooden slats on a cast iron base, has been provided (figure 38). A seating area has also been provided adjacent to the Town Hall and this in turn acts as a physical barrier restricting vehicular access into Bexley Square to one route

The design and implementation of the project was initiated and overseen by the Planning Department. Implementation was carried out by the Direct Works Department between 1983 and 1984 and the maintenance which, to date, has largely consisted of sweep-

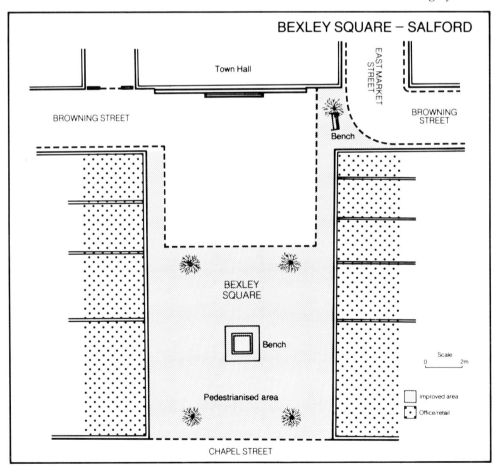

Plan 13: Bexley Square, Salford

Figure 37: Cast iron bollards, Victorian lamposts and semi-mature trees were used as the Square was a conservation area.

Figure 38: New seating close to the Town Hall. The area in front of the Town Hall is to be pedestrianised.

ing, is undertaken by the Environmental Health Department.

Since the completion of the scheme a second phase of works has been proposed for Bexley Square. This will largely consist of an extension of the paved area up to the Town Hall, although this will still allow service vehicle access.

A design deficiency of the original project was the omission of litter bins from the site. This has created problems given the heavy usage of Bexley Square at lunchtime periods and litter bins have subsequently been installed.

The improvements to the square have increased the interest in the adjacent buildings, and in particular the demand for grant aid to improve property. As a result additional finance from the Urban Programme and from private owners has been spent in Bexley Square.

Project schedule – Bexley Square

1980	Policy document prepared by Salford City Council leads to a scheme to visually enhance the built environment along the A6.
1983–84	Closure of Bexley Square to Chapel Street. Pedestrianisation and landscaping project implemented.
1985–86	Provision of litter bins. Proposals to extend pedestrianisation throughout the square.

Costs

The cost of the work undertaken to date in Bexley Square is £38,000 (1983/84) derived from the Urban Programme. This relatively high cost, considering the size of the site, is accounted for by the high quality of design and materials and, in particular, the use of cast iron bollards and lamposts, semi mature trees and

concrete and brick paving. There is no specific budget for maintenance as Bexley Square is cleaned as part of Salford's general street cleaning programme. The lack of any substantial vandalism has meant that, to date, replacement costs have been negligible.

Beneficiaries

The most obvious beneficiaries of the project are those who work in or who use the area regularly, either as a pedestrianised thoroughfare or as a place to stop and rest. The seating areas have proved particularly popular with employees at lunchtimes. Those users interviewed were unanimous in their opinion that the character of the square was enhanced by the project. Noise and air pollution in particular were now noticeably reduced. Most of the users would have preferred more seats due to the popularity of the square, especially in the summer when it serves as a sun trap.

Local traders in the square were, for the most part, complimentary about the project, stating that it had improved their working environment. The majority of traders all said that their businesses had not been affected one way or other in terms of trade as their customers were, in general, long standing. Only one of the traders interviewed thought that trade had fallen due to the loss of passing trade. It was, however, commonly agreed that property values in the Square would benefit from the improvements, and indeed the demand for property in Bexley Square has increased since the completion of the project.

Salford MBC see the Bexley Square project as part of a larger and longer term campaign to improve the image of Salford and to encourage investment. At this stage it is impossible to evaluate the full impact of the project, but the success of Bexley Square suggests that public sector investment along the A6 has helped improve the confidence of local businesses and has encouraged some private sector contributions to the funding of environmental improvement.

109

Voluntary Sector Projects

19   Lever Edge, Bolton

Design features

- New safe access to school.
- Grassing of site.
- Provision of concrete slab footpaths.
- Functional design for minimal maintenance.

Beneficiaries

- Level Edge Primary School.
- Schoolchildren and parents.
- Mancroft Area Residents' Association.
- Lever Edge Labour Club.

Good practice

- Responsive to needs of schoolchildren.
- Parents and children involved in maintenance.
- Low maintenance requirements.
- Community involvement at all stages.
- Meets safety and environmental objectives.

Key facts

Landscaping of a wasteland site adjacent to a school entrance. Provision of a new safer access for school children. Project initiated and partly implemented by the voluntary sector.

Size:		500 square metres.
Cost:	*Capital:*	£5,500 1983/1984.
	Revenue:	Minimal maintenance costs for Parks and Recreation Department, Bolton. Small scale contributions from Parent Teachers Association (less than £100 p.a.).
Funding sources:		Urban Programme £5,000 (capital). Bolton MBC and Lever Edge Primary School PTA (revenue).
Initiator:		Mancroft Area Residents' Association, Lever Edge.
Implementation:		Mancroft Area Residents' Association, Lever Edge. Bolton Task Force (MSC). Local cub scout group.

This project has been selected as an example of good practice in urban environmental improvement not for a particularly innovative or elaborate design but because it was initiated, designed and is partly maintained by a local residents association. The project is also of interest because it has provided a safe access for children to Lever Edge Primary School in Bolton, and because it was implemented and can be maintained at a relatively low cost.

Origins

Owned by Lever Edge Labour Club, this site lies adjacent to the club, and between Lever Edge Primary School and Lever Edge Lane, a main road into the centre of Bolton. The land has been left unmaintained and had attracted tipping. At the same time local residents, through the Mancroft Area Residents' Association and the School's Parent Teacher Association (PTA), began to express their fears about the potential dangers to schoolchildren. At that time the only access into school was through the car park entrance. The school expressed a strong sympathy with these views but, through a lack of resources, was unable to bring about an improvement.

The Residents' Association suggested that, by landscaping the waste site and providing pathways, an eyesore could be removed and a safe access to the school could be provided simultaneously.

The Chairman of Mancroft Area Residents Association took up the initiative towards the end of 1982, approaching first the land owners, the Labour Club, who were found to be enthusiastic and supportive of the idea, but did not have funds to act. Bolton Metropolitan Borough Council were then approached for financial assistance.

Although aware of both the problems of access to the school and the eyesore created by the unmaintained site the local authority had not given remedial action priority. This was partly because the cost of designing, implementing and maintaining the project had been seen as prohibitive. The residents' association proposed that they would prepare a design for the site with a view to minimising the need for maintenance. The Bolton Task Force (a MSC Community Programme Scheme) were approached to provide labour which left Bolton MBC to provide finance for site clearance, materials and a new entrance to the school. Finance from Bolton Metropolitan Borough Council's Urban Programme allocation was approved in June 1983, work was started early in 1984 and was completed within six to seven weeks.

Design, implementation and maintenance

The design drawn up by Mancroft Area Residents' Association had to satisfy three requirements:

(i)   removing the eyesore and providing footpath access to the school;

(ii) maintenance work needed to be minimal and capable of being undertaken by the relatively inexperienced PTA, and by schoolchildren;

(iii) with limited resources the design had to allow for simple, cheap and rapid implementation.

The outcome was a design that was functional, rather than innovative or visually striking. The area of unsightly waste land was replaced by grass (figure 39), with a series of concrete slab pathways linking the pavement to the new school entrance. The new entrance and gateway were provided by the Education Department and were deliberately sited away from the car park entrance and adjacent to the Labour Club (figure 40). A number of small trees and some rose bushes (purchased and planted by the school) were added to enhance the simple design.

Most of the work was undertaken by Bolton Task Force under the supervision of the Residents' Association, but additional help was provided by a local scout

Figure 39: The majority of the site has been grassed, with additional tree and shrub planting.

Figure 40: The new, pedestrian only, access to the school.

group which undertook the planting of the trees and bushes.

The site is maintained by the school through the PTA and by the schoolchildren. Apart from grass cutting, which is undertaken by the Parks and Recreation Department, the local authority are not involved in the maintenance of the site. The reliance on the PTA and school children works reasonably well, although the headmaster expressed some disappointment in the level of support for undertaking maintenance work. Little maintenance work is undertaken during school holidays, which means there are the times of the year when weeds are neglected, but overall the simplicity of the site ensures that there is little that can seriously deteriorate if left unattended for a period of time. One of the most heartening aspects of the project is the relatively low level of vandalism that has taken place, which may be linked to the involvement of local residents, parents and children in the development and care of the project.

Project schedule – Lever Edge

1982	Mancroft Area Residents' Association draw up plans to landscape vacant site at Lever Edge. Bolton MBC approached for finance. Application is made for Urban Programme funding.
1983	Funding Application approved. Bolton Task Force approached to provide necessary labour.
1984	Work undertaken in a six to seven week period.

Costs

Capital costs amounted to £5,500 during 1983/84, and were funded by the Urban Programme. This money was for materials only, as the bulk of the labour requirements were met by the Bolton Task Force. Maintenance costs are low. The Parks and Recreation division of the Environmental Services Department, Bolton MBC cut the grass as part of their general maintenance programme. The PTA make a small annual contribution towards maintenance mainly for tools and weed killer and undertakes some of the maintenance work.

Beneficiaries

The most obvious beneficiaries are the school and its children. A safe access has been provided and the appearance of the site in front of the school dramatically improved. The headmaster expressed pleasure with the outcome of the project and the low level of vandalism. His enthusiasm was only tempered by a slight disappointment at the level of interest in maintenance work.

There are also benefits to the Labour Club who own the site, local residents who overlook it and particularly to members of the Mancroft Area Residents' Association who have gained from active involvement in changing the local environment. Bolton MBC readily admit that without the impetus generated by the Residents' Association it is unlikely that the site would have been improved. Overall, the project demonstrates what can be achieved in terms of small scale environmental improvements at a relatively low cost.

20 Hackney Grove Garden, Hackney

Design features

- Terracing leading towards a performance space.

- A mural with trellis work.

- Stylish blue and green railings.

- Evergreen trees and shrubs for winter cover.

- Details built into the walls and paths.

- Unusual vegetation including eucalyptus and bamboo.

Beneficiaries

- Pre-school children from a nearby nursery.

- Primary school children.

- Psychiatric patients from Hackney Hospital.

- Local community.

- Local employees.

Good practice

- Community involvement in design.

- Sympathetic to needs of local community, and in particular the handicapped, psychiatric patients and school children.

- Educational benefits to children and local residents.

- Involvement of residents and local groups in maintenance.

- Successful and varied planting regime.

- Combination of activities to suit a wide range of users.

- Strong visual impact arising from innovative design.

Key facts

The development of a community garden on a derelict site.

Size: 1,500 square metres.

Cost: Capital: £73,000 (1982–5).

Revenue: £2,000 p.a.

Funding sources: Urban Programme (capital). London Borough of Hackney, (revenue).

Initiator: Local people and London Borough of Hackney.

Implementation: Free Form, a Community Arts Trust, Hackney Grove Garden Group and Artist Contractors.

Origins

Five years ago this secluded, sunken space was all that remained of a burnt-out toy factory. Hackney Council, owners of the half-acre derelict site, whose Housing Department overlooked it, proposed a car park. But local people – both residents and those who worked in premises fronting on to the Grove – had other ideas. They suggested a garden – with special facilities for the elderly and disabled – which could be used by many local groups.

In the autumn of 1981, Free Form, a Community Arts Trust in Hackney with experience of enabling local people to improve their surroundings, was asked to prepare a feasibility study, give technical assistance and cost out the plans. A successful application was made (through Hackney Borough Council) for Inner City Partnership funds of £72,000 over three years to build the garden. A subsequent allocation of £1,000 was made in 1985 to complete the masonry work and provide a fountain in one corner.

During the spring of 1982 Free Form brought together a variety of local organisations and individuals to form the Hackney Grove Garden Group and together they worked on the designs. These early discussions with potential users helped to identify just what was needed. A Dr Barnardo's nursery, housed nearby, had no open space for play. 'Off Centre', a young people's drop-in counselling centre directly opposite the site wanted a place for outdoor activities and volunteered to form a team to help with gardening. Local groups involved in caring for the elderly and disabled wanted opportunities for them to garden. Also in this part of Hackney, with the Housing Department and Town Hall nearby, it was clear that casual use by passers by and space for lunchtime picnickers should be planned for. During this time negotiations took place with the Greater London Council to link the garden to a cycleway running through Hackney Grove.

Design, implementation and maintenance

The overall concept is based upon a gently sloping, curving path (suitable for wheelchairs), which runs through the site (figure 41), finishing at a small level area which can be used for performance. The garden is terraced down from the road to this space, creating a sheltered amphitheatre with many seating areas set amongst boulders and vegetation.

In terms of design, the garden works on two levels: from the outside, where many 'users' in neighbouring offices experience it, and inside.

Outside, from the Grove, the garden appears as an oasis of life and colour beneath the drab walls which enclose it on three sides. In spite of its shaded aspects the image is exotic; careful planting of evergreen trees

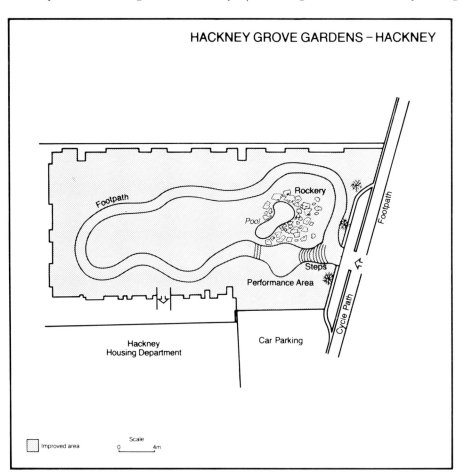

Plan 14: Hackney Grove Garden.

Figure 41: The garden is terraced down towards the small performing area.

Figure 42: The locally built railings at the entrance.

and shrubs gives some winter cover as well as a variety of colour changes throughout the growing season.

Two features dominate the garden from outside – a mural with trellis work on one wall and the stylish blue and green railings which front onto the Grove on either side of the garden's entrance gate. The railings were designed by Free Form in collaboration with an ironsmith who was commissioned to build them (figure 42). They are one of a number of innovative design ideas pioneered in this garden, which have since been used in other community projects on which Free Form has worked. To make the most of the whole space – the garden site and its surroundings – the adjacent Hackney Housing Department was persuaded to refurbish its own car park as part of construction work on the garden. Attractive blue and green railings link the car park and the garden creating a more inviting appearance to those outside the garden.

Inside the garden attention is directed away from the ugly surrounding buildings and onto a rich and amusing variety of detailed features which have been built into the walls and paths. Much has been salvaged from other building sites: a gravestone, masonry faces and other figures. Retaining walls incorporate interesting and unusual brickwork, and a good deal of children's art, including brightly coloured mosaics and clay models. Wooden archways, stone and wooden window frames and doors all enhance the visual diversity and provide opportunities for imaginative and adventurous play (figure 43).

The vegetation is unusual for a small city garden, with much use of eucalyptus, rhododendron and bamboo. This has stood up well to heavy wear and, by suppressing weed growth, is easy to maintain. An award from the 'Shell Better Britain Campaign' will

Figure 43: Wooden archways and brickwork enhance the visual diversity of the garden.

enable a shallow pond and small natural area to be created in the central grassy space.

The work was undertaken under the guidance of Free Form. Artist contractors and craftsmen were brought in and many local people acted as volunteers including psychiatric patients from Hackney Hospital. The garden was substantially complete in two years, at a final cost of £73,000. It is now in daily use. Regular visitors include pre-school children from a nearby nursery, the primary school children, disabled visitors hostel for the handicapped and the psychiatric patients.

At least three times a year there are special garden 'workdays' organised by the Hackney Grove Garden Group who apply each year to Hackney Borough Council for a contribution to garden maintenance and the organisation and publication of celebrations: £2,000 was allocated for 1985/86. Other events – drama and concerts – and a host of more informal activities take place in the performance space. There is little vandalism and litter is cleared frequently by volunteers. Confetti testifies to the garden's increasing use for wedding photographs in a neighbourhood where there are no other green open spaces.

Project schedule – Hackney Grove Garden

Autumn 1981	Free Form asked to prepare feasibility study.
Spring 1982	Hackney Grove Garden Group formed.
1984	Bulk of the work complete.
1985	Completion of masonry work.

Involving the community

From inception to the present, local people have played a major part in the garden. They worked with Free Form on design and with the artist contractors on its creation. There have been frequent celebrations, both during and after the garden was made. Now volunteers maintain it and manage its use.

The role of the Garden Group is crucial both in maintenance and in seeking new ways of extending and sustaining the involvement of local people. Future plans include further planting along a blank wall, sunflower-growing competitions and greater efforts to involve nearby secondary schools – as part of its curriculum – in maintenance and study in the garden.

21   Windmill Hill City Farm, Bristol

Design features

- Farmyard.

- Allotments and garden.

- Nature reserve.

- Cafe and shop.

- Children's play area and playroom.

- All weather sports pitch.

- Adventure playground.

Beneficiaries

- Local residents.

- Volunteers.

- Community Programme workers.

Good practice

- Associated employment and Community Programme posts.

- Educational resource for all age groups.

- Effective re-use of old structures to create new facilities.

- Strong visual impact.

- Community involvement.

- Diversity of funding.

- Continual development.

Key facts

The creation of a city farm in Bristol, one of the earliest examples of its type, which has a number of features designed to cater for a wide range of users .

Size:		18,000 square metres.
Cost:	*Capital:*	£46,000 between 1979 and 1983.
	Revenue:	£7,850 per annum, Bristol City Council. £12,600 (1986), Avon County Council. Finance is also provided by the MSC for a 50 place Community Programme Scheme.
Funding sources:		Urban Programme, £46,000 (capital), 1979–83. Bristol City Council, £7,850 per annum. Avon County Council, £12,600 (1986). Additional funding from the MSC for Community Programme Scheme and revenue from farm activities.
Initiator:		Local residents and the Windmill Hill City Farm Management Committee.
Implementation:		Windmill Hill City Farm Management Committee.

Windmill Hill, one of the earliest city farms in Britain, lies on 1.8 ha. of land which was formerly a scrap yard, in Bedminster, South Bristol. In ten years, the farm has transformed the neighbourhood from a landscape of rubble and abandoned cars to a thriving community centre used and valued by thousands of local people.

In addition to the substantial environmental improvement achieved by the removal of the scrap yard Windmill Hill City Farm is notable for the enthusiasm and involvement it has generated amongst residents and volunteers, without whom the project would not exist. In terms of design the relatively small site has been used imaginatively to provide features that interest, and are used by a wide range of people, from school children to pensioners.

Origins

In the Spring of 1976 a group of local residents objected to Bristol City Council's proposal to use the site (which the council owned) as a high security lorry park. At a popular event organised to gauge local opinion on what should happen, the idea of a city farm emerged and the council agreed to lease the land at a pepper-corn rent for five years. Volunteers began work in 1977, clearing the site, renovating a derelict building (to provide workshop and meeting space) and establishing the farmyard. The first management committee was formed with local people and the farm was registered as a charity. It began to raise funds from trusts and local companies and canvassed for donations of materials to use on the site.

Responding to the needs of the locality the farm started the first of its many community activities – a summer playscheme for local children. Later in the same year the farm took a lead in organising a community bus service in partnership with local councils and a bus company. Residents had been told that it was not possible to provide a normal service on the steep and narrow streets of Windmill Hill.

Figure 44: The farmyard with the barn in the background.

122

Design, implementation and maintenance

The layout of its farm and its activities have developed over a decade in response to community need. Although the farm itself provides the core to the project it is by no means the sole feature of the site. The philosophy behind the design and management of Windmill Hill has been to cater for, and thereby gain the interest and support of, a wide range of the local community. As a result the farm is designed for parents and young children through to teenagers and adults of all ages. There is no set pattern to the planning of the farm but instead it has evolved and adapted to new demands over a period of time.

At present the layout includes a farmyard (figure 44), allotment gardens with an ornamental pond, paddocks for grazing animals, an all weather sports pitch, play spaces for young children, an adventure playground and a nature reserve.

The farm is continually adapting to new demands; raised flower beds for disabled and elderly gardeners are a recent development and herb and butterfly gardens and a tree nursery are under construction. Where possible planting on the farm is designed for visual improvement and to serve other purposes, for example, animal feed, composting, dyeing, and craftwork.

Around the farmyard is a complex of buildings housing farm animals, a playcentre, workshop, a craft and administration space, a cafe, and a dairy. Some, like the playcentre and the cafe, have been purpose-built, but throughout the development of the farm an effort has been made to acquire buildings cheaply: a barn was designed and built by local architectural students, the 'rumpus' playroom was constructed from an old school classroom. Unwanted but useable building materials (such as bricks) are collected from a variety of local sources and stored in a recycling yard on the farm.

In an area of high unemployment with few other community facilities (especially for mothers with young children) the farm offers something for everyone. A playcentre operates throughout the week, with sessions for pre-school children and children who are handicapped. Latest attractions, enjoyed especially by handicapped children, are a computer and the popular 'rumpus room' – a maze of soft, safe foam shapes. There are support groups for new parents and those with handicapped children, for young people and senior citizens. Children's clubs are organised after school and on Saturday mornings, all based on farm activities. The adventure playground and all-weather sports pitch offer supervised facilities for older children and teenagers (figure 45).

Among the farm's most attractive features are the small allotment gardens, let first to those who live in nearby flats, but also used by patients who make regular visits from a psychiatric hospital. A large greenhouse extends the possibilities for horticultural therapy and training (YTS groups have used this) and

Figure 45: There are indoor and outdoor play areas for children of all age groups.

provides plants to stock the gardens and for sale. Here, and in the gardens, there is experiment and research on growing and composting methods.

The farm responds especially well to the needs of women for sociable and creative activity. As well as learning animal husbandry, horticultural and food-processing skills, they can take printing, spinning, weaving and other craft courses or make and repair furniture in a community workshop, which provides tools and guidance for woodwork. This has also been the base for a YTS scheme.

Project schedule – Windmill Hill City Farm

1976	Bristol City Council announce plan to use scrap yard site as a lorry park. Plan dropped in favour of City Farm project.
1977	Work begins on site undertaken by volunteers. Management Committee formed to oversee development of the farm.
1978	First Urban Aid grant for the Farm.
1978–86	City Farm and its funding sources continue to develop. Project continues to develop over time.

Costs

In 1978, an Urban Aid grant paid for a full-time farmer, a workshop organiser and an administrator, and provided £3,000 of capital to establish the farm. In 1983, a further Urban Programme grant of £43,000 was awarded for 3 years to cover building materials and equipment. Bristol City Council continues to let the site at a peppercorn rent and provides grant aid towards staff costs (£7,850 in 1984/5 and in 1985/6). Avon County Council pays for staff members to work with disabled groups in the gardens (£12,600 in 1986).

The cafe, run as a separate enterprise, funds two full-time workers and the farm employs 10 more on permanent jobs (3 full-time). Half of these are supported from the farm's own revenue – fees from a membership of over 600 families, from the weekly activities and courses, the sale of farm produce, and gifts. Links with local firms are strong; the farm benefits from favourable prices and donations of goods – most recently of waste from wholefood shops which cuts the high cost of feeding animals.

Since the farm began, the Manpower Services Commission have funded a number of job creation programmes, and presently support a 50-place Community Programme scheme to help run the farm, its play activities and carry out building work.

Beneficiaries

The residents of the Windmill Hill area and indeed Bristol as a whole have been major beneficiaries of the scheme. The high number of visitors from all age groups and backgrounds indicates the level of interest and employment sustained by the city farm.

There are also those who have benefited from a direct involvement in the scheme. Volunteers, for example, created and in large measure sustain Windmill Hill Farm. They serve on the Management Committee and the seven Area Management Teams through which the farm's different users organise their activities. Volunteers work alongside paid staff and the MSC Community Programme team, both of these groups benefiting from the employment opportunities and community involvement offered by the City Farm.

Overall Windmill Hill is a working model of community resourcefulness. It makes productive use of wasteland, creates a green oasis in the city, offers recreational and educational experiences for all ages and is reaching out in an innovative way to realise the opportunities for community gain.

Part IV

DIRECTORY

Introduction

This directory provides a selection of source material that will be of interest and value to the professional planner, landscape architect, environmental groups and interested individuals alike.

References

Department of the Environment (1986): *Evaluation of Environmental Projects funded under the Urban Programme*, HMSO
An assessment of 173 environmental projects undertaken by JURUE.

Handley and Bulmer P G (1986): *Making The Most of Greenspace*, DoE.
An examination of the maintenance requirements of different landscape improvements.

Books, Brochures, Guides and Reports

Association of Metropolitan Authorities (1985): *Green Policy: A Review of Green Policy and Practice in Metropolitan Authorities*. AMA.

Baines C and Smart J (1984): *A guide to habitat creation*, GLC.
A handbook providing guidance on the creation and management of grasslands, woodlands, wetlands and wastelands in urban areas . Second in the GLC Ecology Handbook series.

Department of the Environment/Environmental Advisory Unit, University of Liverpool (1986): *Transforming our Wasteland: The Way Forward*, HMSO
This book discusses what has happened, what is happening and what can be done about derelict, degraded and neglected land.

Dutton RA and Bradshaw AD (1982): *Land Reclamation in Cities*, HMSO
A manual which explains, from a practical point of view, the ways in which grass, shrubs and trees can be established temporarily or permanently on urban wasteland.

GLC (1984): *Ecology and nature conservation in London*, GLC
A handbook describing the programme of ecological work undertaken by the GLC and providing guidance on ecology in planning and habitat management for planners and environmental groups alike.

GLC (1986): *A Nature Conservation Strategy for London*, GLC
The GLC's Wildlife Habitat Survey identifies the sites which were most important for each of three habitats – wastelands, woodlands and tidal areas. This handbook discusses the criteria for selection and the sites concerned.
(GLC publications are still available from the Greater London Ecology Unit, Room 435, County Hall, London SE1 7PB. (Tel. 01–633–5686)).

Groundwork Foundation (1986): *Community Involvement in Greening Projects*
A study by Christine Bradley of Sheffield University which is concerned with urban greening projects carried out by voluntary organisations and community groups. The study assesses strategies and mechanisms employed by different organisations in executing projects, examines a number of projects in detail and provides models of relationships between voluntary agencies, public authorities and community groups which would alleviate problems of aftercare.

King A and Clifford S (1985): *Holding Your Ground.*
A practical handbook for groups and individuals wishing to become involved with local conservation.

Urban Wildlife Group (n.d): *Nature by Design.*
A teachers' guide to practical conservation which provides a range of material useful for environmental education.

Articles

Special Issue of *Architects Journal* (February 1986): *City Green.*
A selection of articles which consider environmental improvement in cities from a number of different perspectives.

Baines J C: 'Where the grass grows greener'. *Town & Country Planning* 231 September 1983.

Baines J C: 'Success with Plants in Housing Re-Habilitation', *Landscape Design* 4. 1983.

Baines J C: 'Urban Wildlife: a personal view' *Ecos 5 (4)* 1984.

Chandler J (1984): Green London, *Ecos* 5 (4) 1984.

Davidson J: 'In Toxteth's green and pleasant land'. *The Guardian* 1/5/86.

'A whiff of the country'. *The Guardian* 4/9/85.

'The yellowcoats who bring a better world to Oldham'. *The Guardian* 5/3/86.

'Theatrical digs for a plantomime season'. *The Guardian* 2/7/86.

Greening the City: *The Planner* (July 1984).

Contacts

British Trust for Conservation Volunteers
36 St Marys Street
Wallingford
Oxon OX10 0EU

An organisation which has become a central pivot for voluntary action, enabling and equipping other groups and organisations which may wish to undertake practical conservation.

Centre of Urban Ecology
The Birmingham Settlement
318 Summer Lane
Birmingham B19 3RL

An advisory and practical project concerned with the improvement of non-industrial urban wasteland and with educational and social aspects of urban ecology.

CLAWS Ltd
(Community Land and Workspace Services)
61–71 Collier Street
London
N1 9DF

An architectural and design service to voluntary and community groups.

Common Ground
45 Shelton Street
London WC2H 9HJ
01–379–3109

Works to make links between the arts, the conservation of nature and the landscape, with emphasis on the commonplace and everyday aspects of localities.

Community Technical Aid Centre
61 Bloom Street
Manchester
M1 3LZ

CTAC was set up by Manchester City Council and the TCPA in the late 1970's to provide advice and assistance to groups undertaking environmental and community orientated projects.

Free Form, 38 Dalston Lane, London E8 3A2
01–249–3394
An Arts Trust with much experience of enabling communities to improve their neighbourhoods by offering technical advice and assistance.

Groundwork Foundation, Bennetts Court
Bennetts Hill,
Birmingham
021–236–8565

Linking the public, private and voluntary sectors, and with each represented on its board, the Foundation has embarked on its challenging task: 'to improve with and for the benefit of the community the natural and man-made environment within and at the edges of towns, giving emphasis to approaches which create work, jobs and new enterprises and which increase people's sense of responsibility for their surroundings'.

Impact
39 Northumberland Road
Old Trafford
Manchester
M16 9AN

Provides assistance to voluntary groups in the form of tools, machinery and advice.

Landlife
The Old Police Station, Lark Lane,
Liverpool
L17 8UU
051–728–7011

Seeks to involve the community in urban environmental improvement schemes whilst educating, training and creating employment.

London Wildlife Trust
1 Thorpe Close
LONDON
W10 5XL

Aims to promote and protect places of nature conservation interest throughout Greater London, to educate the public in the principles and practice of nature conservation and to carry out surveys and research.

Urban Wildlife Group
11 Albert Street
Birmingham
B4 7YA

Helps local people launch campaigns to conserve and enhance wildlife sites and develops ideas for using nature in education and recreation.

Printed in the United Kingdom for Her Majesty's Stationery Office
Dd.239042. C20. 7/87. 3936. 12521

305001